Vol. 3
Counterattack

BY ABRAHAM ROTHBERG
PICTURES: PIERCE G. FREDERICKS
MICHAEL O'KEEFE
DESIGN: ANTHONY LaROTONDA

BANTAM BOOKS, INC.
NEW YORK / TORONTO / LONDON

contents

EYEWITNESS HISTORY OF WORLD WAR II /
Volume 3: COUNTERATTACK

RLI: | VLM 8 (VLR 7-8)
IL 8-adult

Bantam edition / October 1966;
second printing July 1967; third printing September
1969; fourth printing September 1970; fifth printing
March 1971; sixth printing September 1972; seventh
printing December 1973; eighth printing July 1974;
ninth printing July 1976; tenth printing July 1977.

ISBN 0-553-11307-0

Published simultaneously in the United States
and Canada.

Bantam Books are published by Bantam Books, Inc.
Its trademark, consisting of the words ''Bantam
Books'' and the portrayal of a bantam, is registered
in the United States Patent Office and in other
countries. Marca Registrada. Bantam Books, Inc.,
666 Fifth Avenue, New York, New York 10019.

Printed in the United States of America.

0 9 8 7 6 5 4 3 2 1

1

2

3

The Turning Points

The Battle of Coral Sea

In spring 1942 Japanese conquest reached its high-water mark. The Japanese seemed able to strike anywhere and at will. In April, Nagumo's carriers, which had struck at Pearl Harbor, raided Ceylon, sank two British cruisers and an aircraft carrier, and smashed a large convoy in the Indian Ocean. With Nagumo's force on the loose and the Japanese in control of the Andaman Islands in the Bay of Bengal, Japan might even seize strategically based Madagascar, with the cooperation of the Vichy French, and so control the entire Indian Ocean. On May 5, the British beat them to the punch, storming ashore on Madagascar and seizing the fine harbor of Diego Suarez. By fall they had occupied the entire island.

Doolittle's bombing of the Japanese home islands and the Imperial General Staff's ambition led Japan to try to expand its already swollen orbit still farther to insure the security of its conquests. Extending their perimeter and guarding against Allied air strikes posed a number of objectives for the Japanese: India, Australia, and Hawaii, though none of these was considered an invasion target. But instead of invading India, their forces in Burma knifed into South China's Yunnan Province. At the same time, from the north, their armies drove down into the southwestern prov-

Carrier men using the 40-mm ack-ack gun against Japanese planes.

The carrier Lexington was seriously damaged in the Battle of the Coral Sea.

inces of Chekiang and Fukien to deny airfields there to the Allies. But the Chinese stopped the Japanese in Yunnan only 50 miles up the Salween River, and held them in Fukien and Chekiang.

The chief Japanese effort to expand their outer ring was in the Pacific. If they could enlarge their perimeter to include the Aleutians in the north, Midway in the center, and the Fijis, New Hebrides, New Caledonia, and the Papuan Peninsula in New Guinea in the south, the Japanese could threaten Hawaii and Australia, cut

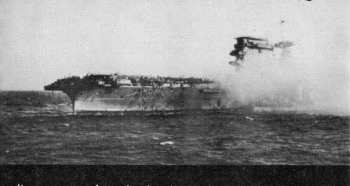

It was necessary for an American destroyer to finish her with torpedos.

American supply lines to Australia, and strengthen their security against Allied attacks. In trying to achieve these goals, the Japanese met their first major setbacks. The Battle of Coral Sea first halted the Japanese tide; the Battle of Midway reversed it.

The Battle of Coral Sea was a five-day aircraft carrier duel from May 4–8, 1942, "the first major engagement in naval history in which surface ships did not exchange a single shot." Fortunately, American intelligence—MAGIC—gave Rear Admiral Frank J.

Fletcher advance information on Japanese plans. They were going to occupy Tulagi in the southern Solomons and send a force around the eastern end of New Guinea to take Port Moresby. The Tulagi landing was made successfully on May 3. The Yorktown's planes arrived the next day, too late to hit the naval escort, but in time to bomb and strafe the Japanese in the harbor. On May 7 the invasion convoy from Rabaul was sighted heading for Port Moresby. American planes immediately attacked and sank part of its escort, the light carrier Shoho. Japanese planes searching for the American carriers sank the U. S. destroyer Sims and the tanker Neosho the same day. But neither Japanese nor U.S. planes sighted each other's main forces. On the next day, American aircraft discovered the main Japanese force and seriously damaged the carrier Shokaku. Its sister ship, Zuikaku, escaped but lost a large number of its planes and pilots in the fray. Japanese planes also spotted the American main force, bombed and torpedoed the carrier Lexington, and damaged the carrier Yorktown.

The Japanese gave as good, or better, than they took at Coral Sea, but they failed in their objective. The Port Moresby invasion convoy was withdrawn and the amphibious assault called off. And, though the Lexington was so badly damaged it was torpedoed and sunk by one of its own escort destroyers, this was kept secret from the Japanese.

Midway

Midway was the decisive naval defeat for the Japanese and the turning point of the war in the Pacific. At the end of May, a great armada of 200 ships, including 11 battleships, 8 aircraft carriers, 22 cruisers, 65 destroyers, 21 submarines, and more than 700 planes, set out from Japan and the Marianas for Midway. The fleet was divided into a carrier striking force under the redoubtable Nagumo, an occupation force under Vice-Admiral Nobutake Kondo, an Aleutians force under Vice-Admiral Boshiro Hosogaya, and the main force under chief of the Imperial Japanese Navy, Admiral Isoroku Yamamoto himself.

Yamamoto's plan was simple. On June 3, Hosogaya would strike at the Aleutians as a diversion, while the rest converged on Midway. There, on June 4, Nagumo's planes would blast Midway, and on June 5, Kondo would invade the small U-shaped atoll which sat in the middle of the Pacific. If and when the American fleet could be lured into a counterattack, Yamamoto's powerful and speedy battleships, held back out of the range of American aircraft, would pounce on it and annihilate it. Once an advanced airbase was established on Midway, it could be used to reduce American carrier strikes in the South and Central Pacific, and eventually provide a springboard for invading Hawaii.

Yamamoto's plan needed surprise for success, but once more MAGIC's cracking of the Japanese code gave Admiral Chester W. Nimitz the general outlines of the scheme and he was able to prepare for it. After reinforcing Midway Island itself with as many planes, guns, and men as he could lay hands on, Nimitz built two task forces around his only three carriers. Task Force 16 under Rear Admiral Raymond Spruance had the carriers Enterprise and Hornet, 6 cruisers, and 9 destroyers. Task Force 17 and over-all command were under Rear Admiral Fletcher, who had the Yorktown (its three months' worth of damage sustained in the Coral Sea battle miraculously repaired by 48 hours of non-stop work at Pearl Harbor), 2 cruisers, and 7 de-

Although the American torpedo planes were slaughtered at the Battle of Midway — only one man returned from Torpedo Squadron 8 — their attack pulled the Japanese fighter cover low and permitted American dive bombers (above) to make their attack opposed only by anti-aircraft fire. The dive bombers hit four carriers and the heavy cruiser Mogami (below). Loss of the carriers and pilots cost the Japanese the initiative at sea.

stroyers. Nimitz deployed both task forces north of Midway from where he expected Nagumo to strike.

On June 2, Hosogaya's diversionary force bombed Dutch Harbor in the Aleutians, and the next day, Nagumo's carriers were sighted 200 miles northwest of Midway. They had already launched their planes against Midway. Midway's planes took off immediately —bombers and torpedo planes to attack the carriers, fighters to intercept the Japanese bombers. But the obsolete American fighters were no match for the speedy Zero escort. The Japanese bombers got through, plastering the island; but, incredibly, they did not damage the main installations: the air strip, the radar, and the radio. The Zeros protecting Nagumo's task force also shot almost every one of the American torpedo plane and dive-bomber attackers out of the sky before a single hit could be scored on a Japanese ship.

On the morning of June 4 the opposing carrier forces discovered each other and immediately launched their planes. Of the 41 torpedo planes sent against them, the Japanese shot down 35, and not a single torpedo found its mark. But U. S. planes had attacked with such reckless bravery that they engaged both enemy fighters and anti-aircraft, and the Enterprise's dive bombers were able to get through to smash two carriers, the Kaga and Soryu, and the Yorktown's to leave Nagumo's flagship carrier, the Akagi, a flaming hulk. Captain Mitsuo Fuchida, the Japanese Naval Air Force officer who had led the Pearl Harbor attack, was on the Akagi when the U.S. dive bombers struck.

One after another, planes were hoisted from the hangar and quickly arranged on the flight deck. There was no time to lose. At 10:20 Admiral Nagumo gave the order to launch when ready. On Akagi's flight deck all planes were in position with engines warming up.

15

Within five minutes all her planes would be launched.

Five minutes! Who would have dreamed that the tide of battle would shift completely in that brief interval of time?

Visibility was good. Clouds were gathering at about 3000 meters, however, and though there were occasional breaks, they afforded good concealment for approaching enemy planes. At 10:24 the order to start launching came from the bridge by voice-tube. The Air Officer flapped a white flag, and the first Zero fighter gathered speed and whizzed off the deck. At that instant a lookout screamed, 'Hell-divers!' I looked up to see three black enemy planes plummeting toward our ship. Some of our machine guns managed to fire a few frantic bursts at them, but it was too late. The plump silhouettes of the American 'Dauntless' dive bombers quickly grew larger, and then a number of black objects suddenly floated eerily from their wings. Bombs! Down they came straight toward me! I fell intuitively to the deck and crawled behind a command post mantelet.

The terrifying scream of the dive bombers reached me first, followed by the crashing explosion of a direct hit. There was a blinding flash and then a second explosion, much louder than the first. I was shaken by a weird blast of warm air. There was still another shock, but less severe, apparently a near-miss. Then followed a startling quiet as the barking of guns suddenly ceased. I got up and looked at the sky. The enemy planes were already gone from sight.

The attackers had gotten in unimpeded because our fighters, which had engaged the preceding wave of torpedo planes only a few minutes earlier, had not yet had time to regain altitude. Consequently, it may be said that the American dive bombers' success was made possible by the earlier martyrdom of their torpedo planes. Also, our carriers had no time to evade because clouds hid the enemy's approach until he dove down to the attack. We had been caught flatfooted in the most vulnerable condition possible — decks loaded with planes armed and fueled for an attack.

Looking about, I was horrified at the destruction that had been wrought in a matter of seconds. There was a huge hole in the flight deck just behind the amidship elevator. The elevator itself, twisted like molten glass, was dropping into the hangar. Deck plates reeled upward in grotesque configurations. Planes stood tail up, belching livid flame and jet-black smoke. Reluctant tears streamed down my cheeks as I watched the fires spread, and I was terrified at the prospect of induced explosions which would surely doom the ship. . . .

I could see that the Kaga and Soryu had also been hit and were giving off heavy columns of black smoke. The scene was horrible to behold.

In the meantime, Nagumo's sole remaining carrier, Hiryu, launched its planes against the Yorktown and hit the U. S. carrier with bombs and torpedoes. In swift reprisal American dive bombers from the Enterprise left the Hiryu limping and aflame, to be given the coup de grace by Japanese destroyers. Two days later, the Yorktown, still afloat and being helped by the destroyer Hammann, was sunk together with the Hammann by a Japanese submarine.

After battling three days and nights, with his carriers at the bottom, Yamamoto broke off the engagement on June 6 and ordered his armada to withdraw. Though his diversionary force took Attu, Kiska, and Adak in the western Aleutians on June 7–8, Yamamoto had suffered the greatest naval defeat in Japanese

Shortly before a vast Japanese armada descended on Midway, the Navy deciphered their instructions and stationed Admiral Spruance north and east of the enemy trap. It was the only advantage Spruance had—his carrier force was small. Nevertheless, the Americans were able to inflict the greatest defeat in Japanese naval history: 4 carriers, 2 cruisers, 275 planes, and 4800 men were lost.

Firefighters (above) on the Yorktown (left) fought to save the ship and it seemed that they were to be successful. A destroyer began to tow her back to Pearl Harbor. Then a Japanese submarine hit her with a torpedo. It was a small loss compared with the enemy losses in ships and pilots.

history. He had lost his best 4 carriers, their irreplaceable crack pilots, 2 heavy cruisers, some 275 planes, and more than 4800 men. The bitterest loss of face was that he had lost the battle to a weaker fleet.

The United States lost the Yorktown, the Hammann, 150 planes and 307 men, but Midway remained in American hands. The Japanese threat was now over, the initiative had shifted to the United States.

Covered by a smoke screen, Australians attack a desert strong point.

The Desert War

Victory in the desert depended primarily on which side could more rapidly replenish its supplies, reinforce its troops and replace its armor before a decisive battle was fought. The British supply route ran 3000 miles and three months around the Cape of Good Hope to Suez; the Afrika Korps' only 300 miles and three days across the Mediterranean from Italy to Tripoli. At the end of 1941, as both Rommel and Auchinleck prepared offensives, the German supply situation was critical. The RAF and Royal Navy based on Malta were slashing Axis convoys to Rommel so badly that by October only one ship in four was getting to Tripoli. Auchinleck was, therefore, able to strike first. In two months, he thrust forward all the way to El Agheila in western Cyrenaica, relieving Tobruk and driving Rommel before him, but unable to encircle and annihilate Rommel's striking power.

As Rommel fell back, the Germans, in November, transferred 25 submarines from the Atlantic to the Mediterranean and in December diverted an entire air group from the Russian front to Sicily and North Africa. Together these wrested command of the sea and air from the British, battered Malta and neutralized that thorn in the side of Axis supply lines. The British were unable to stop a single Axis convoy in January and, in turn, in attempting to send food, fuel, and planes to beleaguered Malta suffered grievous losses. The aircraft carrier Ark Royal, the battleship Barham, the cruisers Neptune and Galatea, were sent to the bottom. On December 18, the battleships Queen Elizabeth and Valiant were put out of action in Alexandria harbor by Italian "human torpedoes." The hard-pressed Eastern Mediterranean Fleet was left with 3

The British infantry fought from foxholes and from behind abandoned tanks

cruisers and 6 destroyers.

With his supplies flowing through unimpeded, Rommel counterattacked on January 21, 1942. Though inferior in numbers and almost without air support, the Desert Fox drove the British back 350 miles to El Gazala in 17 days of fierce fighting. By then, his supply lines extended and hammered by the RAF, he paused to regroup. While both sides tried to refit, the British attempted to push convoys through to Malta so that the island could once more take its toll of Axis convoys to the Afrika Korps, but the Luftwaffe and the U boats kept the island so tightly blockaded that almost no ships got through. In the attempt, the British lost 2 cruisers, the Naiad and Hermione, and 4

to hold off the Rommel offensive which threatened to break through to Suez.

destroyers. In April 1 the Luftwaffe mauled Maltese port installations so badly that British naval vessels had to leave at the end of the month.

With his supply lines open, Rommel renewed his offensive on May 26. Outflanking Bir Hacheim, the southern anchor of Auchinleck's Gazala defense line, Rommel's armor lunged north at Tobruk, threatening to cut off a large part of the Eighth Army. At the same time, Rommel's tanks and the Luftwaffe pounded the Free French and Jewish Battalion at Bir Hacheim. After two weeks of bitter resistance, General Pierre Koenig was forced to evacuate Bir Hacheim on June 10. Three days later, when Rommel trapped and wiped out 230 of 300 British tanks counterattacking his flank, the

Rommel—"The Desert Fox"—(above) and General Montgomery (below) who was assigned to put the Eighth Army over to the offensive after Rommel had been stopped at Alam Halfa. (Right) Nazi artillery scores a near-miss.

catastrophe was certain. To avoid encirclement, the British pulled back to Mersa Matruh, once again leaving a garrison at Tobruk to harass Rommel's communications. In a two-day lightning assault, combining tanks, artillery, and dive bombers, Rommel reduced Tobruk on June 21 and captured 33,000 men as well as huge quantities of supplies. The debacle was almost completed.

Rommel raced across the Egyptian border and by June 29 had taken Matruh and forced Auchinleck to retreat another 120 miles to prepared positions at El Alamein, only 70 miles from Alexandria. Here, with only a 40-mile defense line from the sea to the impassable sands of the Quattara Depression, Auchinleck could not be outflanked, and, reinforced with fresh troops, tanks and planes, the battered and weary Eighth Army stood fast. The entire catastrophic campaign from Gazala to Alamein had cost the Eighth half its manpower and much of its heavy equipment.

With his troops worn-out and his supply lines overextended Rommel paused to rest and regroup in July. But at the end of August, the daring Desert Fox made one more brilliant attempt to breach the Alamein defenses and break into the Nile Delta. An Afrika Korps spearhead drove through British positions to a depth of 25 miles before it was stopped, chiefly by savage RAF strikes up and down Rommel's lines from forward columns to rear bases.

The entire campaign had been such a stunning defeat, and still posed such a pregnant threat to Suez, that Prime Minister Churchill himself flew from England to Egypt in August to shake up the Middle East leadership. General Sir Harold Alexander was appointed to replace Auchinleck in over-all command, and Lieutenant General Bernard L. Montgomery was given tactical control of the Eighth Army. It was to prove a fateful change; Rommel was to meet his match.

Stalingrad

What limited Rommel's supplies and consequently his victories was Hitler's concentration of most of his armor and aircraft on the vast Russian front. In December 1941, when his armies ground to a halt before Moscow, Hitler refused to give up any of the territory by retreating to winter quarters. Instead, since the front was too huge to set up a continuous defense line of trenches, Hitler permitted them to garrison various communications centers, usually cities astride the main railways, which the Wehrmacht ringed with steel. The Germans called these fortified areas Igels, or "hedgehogs," because they bristled with guns. Here they were able to weather both cold and Russian winter counter-offensives, before resuming the attack in spring 1942. The Russian counterattacks continued, striking at the hedgehogs, and Heinrich Haape, a Wehrmacht doctor, told of one in the Moscow sector:

The Russian artillery stopped at about 5 A.M. and we heard a screaming mob coming towards us from the east again. Their high-pitched 'Oorair! Oorair!' came across the snow to us. On they came towards the barn, yelling and screaming at the top of their voices. A flare picked them out—a close-packed body of charging men. From our holes in the snow and our wooden barricades behind the dressing station we fired our automatics and rifles into the advancing mass. They went down by the dozen, but the men behind trod the bodies into the snow. They took the Kolkhoz barn again, but this time we fired grenades into the barn, where the Russians were still kicking up an infernal din. Some of the Reds charged out of the barn right into the muzzles of our guns. Confused hand-to-hand fighting developed, but suddenly the mass of Russians in the barn took to their heels and fled.

Cautiously some of our men entered the barn. There were dead and wounded Russians littering the floor, victims of the grenades. But in a corner were two Russians singing raucously, quite oblivious of what was going on around them. Then it dawned on us—the Russians were blind drunk! From the less seriously wounded we gathered that the commissars, becoming desperate at the Red Army's inability to break through our lines in night attacks, had issued their troops with generous rations of alcohol, and when all the men were

thoroughly drunk, had launched the attack!

Although the Russians persisted in their counter-attack, they achieved only minor victories, the most important of which was some relief of beleaguered Leningrad by building a highway across frozen Lake Ladoga. Alexander Werth, Russian-born British journalist, saw Leningrad's grim suffering during that siege.

Most of these people pulled themselves together when they were given work. It was a great thing. But on the whole men collapsed more easily than women and at first the death-rate was highest among the men. However, those who survived the worst period of the famine finally survived. The women felt the after-effects more seriously than the men. Many died in the spring when the worst was already over. The famine had peculiar physical effects on people. Women were so run down that they stopped menstruating ... so many people died that we had to bury most of them without coffins. People had their feelings blunted, and never seemed to weep at the burials. It was all done in complete silence without any display of emotion. When things began to improve the first signs were when women began to put rouge and lipstick on their pale skinny faces. Yes, we lived through hell right enough; but you should have been here the day the blockade was broken — people in the streets wept for joy and strangers fell around each other's necks. ...

One of the greatest examples of how Leningrad fought for its life was when in the spring 300,000 to 400,000 people came out into the street with shovels — people who could scarcely stand on their feet, so weak and hungry were they — and proceeded to clean up the town. All winter the drains and sewers had been out of action; there was a great danger of epidemics spreading with the coming of warm weather. And in a few

days these 300,000 or 400,000 weak, hungry people — many of them were very old people who had never handled a shovel in their lives — had shovelled away and dumped into the river and the canals all those mountains of snow and filth which, had they remained there, would have poisoned Leningrad. And it was a joy to see the city streets a few days later all clean and tidy. It had a great moral effect.

In the spring, Hitler, who had assumed personal command on the Eastern Front, moved from his East Prussian "Wolf's Lair" headquarters to Vinnitsa in the Ukraine. The purposes and strategy of the Nazi offensive of 1942 differed greatly from those of 1941, and Hitler was on hand to supervise their attainment personally. Instead of decimating the Russian armies and capturing Moscow, the Führer now tried to strangle Russia's war effort by cutting off its strategic resources. The primary targets, the Donets Basin, the Caucasian oil fields, and the Volga Valley, would deprive the Russians of essential supplies of food, industrial products, and mineral wealth. Most important, if the Germans could take the Caucasian and Caspian oil fields, they would get some 30,000,000 tons of oil a year for their planes and Panzers and deny it to the Red Army. Strategically, the Caucasus would provide a land bridge over which Hitler's legions could pour into Iran, severing the flow of Anglo-American aid to Russia and isolating Turkey. They might even go further, south into India to join hands with Japan, and west through the oil-rich Mosul Basin in Iraq to join hands with the Afrika Korps thrusting east through Egypt. In taking Stalingrad, the key to the Volga Valley, they would also cut the Volga River, one of the last remaining north-south communication lines west of the Urals still in Russian hands.

Russian cities and villages were burned to the ground as they came in the path

Tactically, the first step was to clear the Crimea, securing the German right flank, then to capture Rostov, so that the Panzers could wheel southeast into the Caucasus. On May 8, General Fritz von Mannstein opened the offensive against Kerch in the Crimea. Four days later, Timoshenko, striving to throw the Germans' timetable out of kilter and divert their impending plunge toward Stalingrad and the Caucasus, hurled his divisions against Kharkov from the south. By May 18 the Red Army had driven into the suburbs of Kharkov. The Germans then launched a violent

of the German offensive. Civilians starved in the land of the scorched earth.

counterattack which threw the Russians back with heavy losses. By June 1 they were ready to resume the offensive. On June 5, von Mannstein blasted Sevastopol and after a month-long stubborn Russian resistance, the grim six-month siege of the city was over. Boris Voyetekhov told what the city's final agony was like:

When we at last reached the inner harbor we saw Sevastopol enveloped in the flame and smoke of fires set by German incendiaries. The fascist knife was at the unhappy city's very throat....

There is no town left. The houses are all roofless, the streets are nearly all blocked by avalanches of rubble.

There was no place in the town where instruments of death did not prevail. No place was safe from bombs, land mines, or shellfire. Everything that moved — cutters, cars and motorcycles — was pursued and attacked. Enemy air squadrons sought out women and children who were sheltering among the rocks, await-

The Nazi troops and tanks drove ahead through southern Russia, but this left

ing their turn to be evacuated. Powerful explosives buried them in the debris beside the sea.

Every day the divers reported to the Admiralty commissar about material recovered from the bottom of the harbor. These experts in underwater mysteries dived every night and, amid old wrecks and skeletons of the dead, they loaded their baskets with unexploded bombs and shells.

The commissar was insatiable. He carefully thumbed

a vulnerable flank to be attacked in the Red Army's winter offensive.

rescued bills of lading, asking persistently: "Where are those 6 airplane engines? Where are the bandages, the cotton, wool and drugs? What are you doing there? Playing chess with the dead?"

"Just that," replied the chief diver, "and you had better take a hand down below; then you will be satisfied that it is impossible to get up those motors. They are covered with piles of dead horses and cavalrymen in the hold. Drugs"—he hesitated—"I can't go there."

"Why not?"

"I have been a diver for 30 years. I have seen things that drove people who were working next to me mad, but to go into that cabin where, if I open the door, dead bodies of children will rush toward me—no, I can't."

"Well," said the commissar, "that means you are letting living children die for lack of food and bandages."

The discussions always ended with the divers going back down below. And in the morning the airplane motors were taken to the airfield, and the bandages were drying in the sun, and the salvaged shells were on the way to the enemy through Sevastopol's sky.

Night after night our ships would steal into the harbor bringing reinforcements and supplies, evacuating women and children. The Germans illuminated the landing stages with parachute flares and searchlights, and shelled them unmercifully. The scene was indescribable: oil tanks blazed; cases of ammunition exploded; truck drivers rushed overloaded machines through the flame and smoke while the fire-fighters strove to check the fires.

Always there was the effort to maintain the tremendous tempo of loading and unloading. Faster, faster, faster. At dawn every vessel must be far away from the quay. The stakes were high and the methods used had to be ruthless. Among the dock laborers were a number of convicts. One of them had organized a group of malcontents who delayed the work. A communications officer came up to the convict leader and said: "Open your mouth and say 'Ah!'" Whereupon he shot the man in the teeth, spattering those around with blood and brains. Then turning to the others, he said, "I want tempo. . . ."

Within the city there was no time for funerals. The dead were covered with a thin layer of earth. On a hillock, where a damaged plane lay, I read these words written on a piece of a propeller: "Make room, you in the graves. Shift, you old soldiers. A newcomer has joined you to prove his love of battle. Take him into your graves. He is worthy."

When Sevastopol fell, the Germans captured 90,000 prisoners and took vast quantities of supplies.

After a two-day battle the Russians evacuated Rostov on June 27 and the Nazi spearheads were free to drive through the Kuban into the Caucasus. By August 8, General Siegmund List and General Ewald von Kleist's Panzers had occupied the Maikop oil fields which the Russians had left "scorched earth." On September 10, Nazi forces had captured the naval base of Novorossisk and the Red Black Sea Fleet had to retreat again, this time to Tuapse. Though on August 25 their men had planted the swastika on Mount Elbrus, the highest peak in the Caucasus, fuel shortages and transfer of some of their forces to the attack on Stalingrad left Kleist's legions still more than 300 miles from the main Russian oil fields at Baku. Hitler had failed to gain his first objective.

In the other wing of the Nazi offensive, General Friedrich Paulus's 6th Army in the 2 months between

The Russians fought gallantly within the city of Stalingrad.

late June and September 1 had advanced 300 miles, into the outskirts of Stalingrad. Because Hitler was sure Russian resistance before Stalingrad was broken and the city's fall imminent, he had diverted a considerable portion of Paulus's planes and tanks to help Kleist in the Caucasus. Before he could bring them back north, the Russians were entrenched and fighting fiercely in defense of Stalingrad and it was too late.

Initially, Hitler's generals tried to persuade him to concentrate on either Stalingrad or the Caucasus, rather than dividing German striking power on fronts and against objectives 350 miles apart. But Hitler overruled them. In addition, after Mannstein stormed Sevastopol, Hitler sent his forces and equipment to Leningrad to see if they could repeat the performance. Moreover, in August, after the Canadian raid on Dieppe, Hitler's fear of a second front in the West caused him

Civilians were either evacuated or put to work on defenses.

to transfer some of his Russian army units to France, thus weakening his concentrations before Stalingrad even further. But most important of all, the Nazis had never been able to take Voronezh, and thereby had exposed a long northern flank, poorly defended by Hungarian, Italian, and Romanian divisions. Here the Russian blow was to fall.

Instead of outflanking Stalingrad by crossing the Volga River and cutting it off, Hitler chose to take the city by storm. Though Stalingrad was almost completely leveled by Nazi artillery and aerial bombardment, bitter nand-to-hand, house-to-house, and street-to-street fighting went on in the ruins for 2 months until, by the first week in November, most of Stalingrad was in the invaders' hands.

Then came Russia's winter cold and snow and on November 19 the Red Army went over to the attack.

Heinz Schroter described the Russian offensive:

At midnight it began to snow.

The temperature dropped to −6° centigrade, and visibility to nil. The weather, in fact, was atrocious. Once again "General Winter" was clearly on the side of the Red Army. . . .

Like a blast on a trumpet, the battle began. The time was 4 o'clock in the morning. The "God of War," as Stalin had called the artillery, beat an awful tattoo. For 4 hours 800 guns and mortars rained fire and steel on the German and Rumanian positions. Where the shells landed, sand, beams, girders, were hurled high in the air, pillboxes were torn apart like card houses, and fountains of earth leaped from the ground. A white hot wall of flame and steel moved over the land.

The lunar landscape bore a strange crop of fiery, scarlet mushrooms. Branches, legs, beams, bodies, bits of metal, rifles, clods of earth, platoons, companies, battalions, regiments, were buried under the snow and mud, or hurled high in the air. A belt of ground 2 miles deep was turned into a blazing inferno.

At 8 o'clock the tanks came.

The air was heavy with the thunder of their engines, and the rattle of steel against steel. The terror that had been hidden was approaching fast.

The gray curtains of fog came to life.

The Russian tanks advanced, wave after wave, as though on parade. Anti-tank grenades ripped gaping holes in their flanks. Hundreds of tanks became smoking ruins, hundreds were blown up by mine or shell. Gaps appeared in the Russian ranks, but still they came on.

They struck at the Hungarians, Italians, and Romanians guarding the extended Nazi northern flank and broke through. Reinforced by fresh Siberian tanks,

November 19 — the Russians opened an offensive against the Germans.

Red Army men charge through the snow as the Nazi lines begin to crack.

supported by massed artillery, 3 Russian armies drove spearheads from the north and south into the exhausted Axis flanks. Within 4 days they had encircled 300,000 men in a pocket 25 miles long from east to west, and 12 miles·wide from north to south. Trapped between the Don and Volga Rivers were 20 German and 2 Romanian divisions of the crack 6th Army.

General Franz Halder, Chief of the German General Staff, had warned Hitler so insistently of that weak flank that finally in September he had been replaced

Red Army tanks and infantry encircled 300,000 Axis troops at Stalingrad.

by General Kurt Zeitzler. Halder had also cautioned Hitler that the Russians had 1,500,000 men in reserve for a counteroffensive and were producing twice as many tanks every month as the Germans. Hitler replied: "Spare me this idiotic nonsense. The Russians are finished. In 4 weeks' time they will collapse."

Now, the generals called for Paulus to fight his way westward out of the trap, but Hitler refused to countenance retreat from the Volga. "Where the German soldier once sets his foot," the Führer orated, "there

Hitler refused to permit General von Paulus to retreat from the Volga River.

he remains and no power on earth will drive him back."
Hitler was as much hypnotized by his own words as by
what the Nazis had taken in little more than a year in
Russia. They controlled more than a third of Russia's
people, more than half its coal, aluminum, manganese,
iron ore, electrical power, 40 per cent of its food,
railroads, and machine tool production, and more than
a third of its chemical industry.

The generals pleaded for a force to break through

As December wore on, the weather around Stalingrad turned bitterly cold and

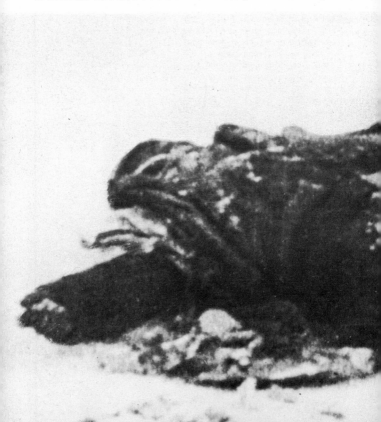

to relieve the 6th Army, but Hitler dallied. By the time he permitted Mannstein to attempt a breakthrough in mid-December, it was too late. Benno Zeiser, fighting against the tightening Russian ring, wrote:

The truth was slowly borne in on us, as, dragging all they had with them, the remnants of defeated division after division fell back from all sides before the on-pressing enemy, crowding and cramming into the heart of the cauldron. Gradually the columns of

the snow was driven by fierce winds. German wounded froze where they lay.

converging transport blocked all roads. . . . Vast supplies of provisions and clothing had to become huge
fireworks, not to fall into enemy hands. Installations
erected at enormous effort were wiped out wholesale.
The country for miles around was strewn with smaller
equipment — tin-hats, gas-masks in cases, ground-
sheets, cooking utensils, ammo pouches, trenching
tools, even rifles, machine-pistols, and grenades. All
of this stuff had been thrown away because it had
become a mere hindrance, or because the men who
carried it had become the wounded in their endless
columns, with blood-soaked bandages and tattered
uniforms, summoning the last vestiges of their strength
merely to drag themselves on through the snow. Or
else the equipment had belonged to the countless men
now rigid and dead, of whom nobody took any more
notice than we did of all that abandoned material.

Completely cut off, the men in field gray just
slouched on, invariably filthy and invariably louse-
ridden, their weary shoulders sagging, from one defense
position to another. The icy winds of those great white
wastes which stretched for ever beyond us to the east
lashed a million crystals of razor-like snow into their
unshaven faces, skin now loose-stretched over bone,
so utter was the exhaustion, so utter the starvation. It
burned the skin to crumpled leather, it lashed tears
from the sunken eyes which from over-fatigue could
scarce be kept open, it penetrated through all uniforms
and rags to the very marrow of our bones. And when-
ever any individual could do no more, when even the
onward-driving lash of fear of death ceased to have
meaning, then like an engine which had used its last
drop of fuel, the debilitated body ran down and came
to a standstill. Soon a kindly shroud of snow covered
the object and only the toe of a jackboot or an arm

frozen to stone could remind you that what was now an elongated white hummock had quite recently been a human being. . . .

In spite of all this we still again and again experienced sheer astonishment when we saw that we were not the only ones whom death had spared for the time being, that there was still much tenacious life in this inferno of bellowing steel, and that that life was manifesting itself now even at that moment by sending red and violent flares into the heavens, warning of attack, warning of tanks, and urgent cries for help. And then we fired straight into the storming yelling mass of Bolsheviks, and fired automatically as robots until at last the mammoth tanks, clattering down on us, compelled yet another withdrawal farther back still into the cauldron which with every day grew smaller.

Göring had supported Hitler's decision to have Paulus stand fast and boastfully promised his Air Force would supply the encircled 6th Army. The Luftwaffe made extraordinary efforts but bad weather and withering Russian fire made a failure of the airlift. Refused permission to break out, unable to be relieved, reinforced, or even adequately supplied with food, fuel, and ammunition, the 6th Army stubbornly fought on. Though the Russians offered Paulus surrender terms to avoid further useless slaughter, Hitler denied him permission to submit. The best the Führer could offer was verbal assurance, in New Year's greetings to the 6th Army: "You have my word that everything will be done to deliver you," and to insist that Paulus go on fighting to the bitter end.

It came 7 desperate weeks later when, after being cut into two parts, the 6th Army finally surrendered on January 31, and February 2, 1943. Of almost 300,000 men, only 90,000 remained alive for the Red

The German Sixth Army at Stalingrad surrendered at the end of January, 1943. General von Paulus (above) had only 90,000 troops left out of his original force of 300,000.

Army to take, with mountains of equipment, in the most catastrophic defeat a German Army had suffered.

The Stalingrad victory imperiled German penetrations into the Caucasus. If the Russians recaptured Rostov, all Kleist's forces there would also be cut off. Reluctantly, Hitler permitted them to be withdrawn.

Not only had Hitler made disastrous military errors in the campaign, he also committed catastrophic political mistakes. As he neglected to encourage the widespread discontent in the Ukraine during his 1941 campaign, he now ignored the political unrest he found among Cossacks, Caucasians, Moslems, Crimean Tatars, and Kalmuks. Nor did the Führer properly utilize Russian deserters who had been recruited into a volunteer anti-Communist army under General Vlasov. Most important, Nazi Schrecklichkeit alienated most of those Russians hostile to the Soviet regime.

Nazis inspecting the wreckage of a train derailed by the Norwegians.

The Russians learned more from their military and political experience. The disaffected minorities were wooed by a major propaganda campaign in October 1942 which exalted the heroic role minority nationalities had played in the war. Red Army defeats caused a ruthless purge of its ranks. Younger officers were elevated to command; and the Presidium eliminated the "dual command" system by abolishing political commissars.

Underground Resistance

Wherever a Nazi set his jack boot down, persecuting and plundering his victims, a crop of hatred sprouted and resistance grew. At first prostrate beneath the invader's heel, Nazi-occupied Europe soon hit back. In most countries, the frightened majority either pas-

sively collaborated or passively resisted, but there were also the committed minorities. At one extreme were the Nazi collaborators—the Quislings, Lavals, Degrelles, Seyss-Inquarts, and their ilk—who helped build and bolster the New Order. At the other end were those courageous few who despised and fought Nazism's brutal tyranny. Some fought as individuals and some as organized groups, everywhere committed to espionage, sabotage, and outright military action, and always at the risk of savage reprisal: the concentration camp, torture, death.

While Hitler forcibly impressed 5,000,000 slave-laborers and systematically looted occupied Europe of its wealth and produce, as the Nazi mass extermination

The well-organized units of the French underground (below) blew trains, helped downed Allied airmen to escape, and even passed intelligence along to England. German counter-intelligence inflicted heavy casualties on the underground.

campaign of the Jews sent millions up in smoke, underground conspirators anonymously delivered their small but telling blows. Trains were derailed, tracks blown up, bridges dynamited, telephone wires slashed, warehouses burned, machinery sabotaged. Newspapers were published and distributed, essential information passed on to the Allies, arms were secreted, collaborators were punished, and German patrols ambushed. In many areas, particularly Poland, Yugoslavia, and Greece, the Nazis met armed uprisings and implacable partisan warfare.

If many individuals fought for dubious motives and in questionable ways, if resistance groups of differing political persuasions too often were more intent on slaughtering one another than on resisting the enemy, these were the malignant results of conquest and chaos, and of the frailty and confusion that beset mankind. Nonetheless, as Winston Churchill wisely noted in July 1941, "The V sign is the symbol of the unconquerable will of the occupied territories, and a portent of the fate awaiting the Nazi tyranny. So long as the peoples of Europe continue to refuse all collaboration with the invader, it is sure that his cause will perish, and that Europe will be liberated."

In what seems like a commonplace incident — most resistance had to be undramatic — Colonel Remy describes a typical illustration of heroic underground action:

In November 1941, Espadon had given me in Paris a blade of metal, about the size of two postage stamps.

"Send it off to London," he requested, "it's the sample they asked for by wireless."

I turned the little blade over in my hand. The metal of which it was made seemed extraordinarily light and very hard. It was of a bluish-grey colour.

"I reported to London," Espadon informed me, "that the S.N.C.A.S.O. factory at Bordeaux was making this metal in great secrecy on behalf of the Luftwaffe."

"Yes," I told him, "I read your report. You said there that the Germans were taking extraordinary precautions against any leakage of the material through the work people; that they were obliged to take off their clothes and put on special overalls which had the hems unsewn; that they were very carefully searched when they left the factory, and that they were obliged to wash their hands and brush their nails in case they took away even the tiniest particle or filing that way."

"That's right."

"How did you manage to get hold of this bit, then?"

"Do you remember," he recounted, "that on II November, five minutes of silence was observed everywhere, together with a general stoppage or slowing down of work, according to the request General de Gaulle made over the radio? In the S.N.C.A.S.O. factory all the workpeople downed tools, except one who went on working as if there was nothing unusual on. When the five minutes were up, all his neighbours turned on him, and knocked him down. The Germans intervened, and the man, who had fainted, was carried home. The next day I had the piece of metal."

"So it was he . . ." I concluded his story for him.

"Yes, he was one of our men. I had asked him for the sample. He had heard the general's order and had said to himself that the attention of the Germans would be entirely occupied with those who stopped working. He was wearing clogs, underneath which were fixed strips of rubber cut off from old motor tires. Many of them do that. On the morning of 11 November, he managed to cut off a piece of metal the right size. When the others downed tools, he went on working and let this piece fall to the ground without the Germans noticing. By pushing his foot against the bench he managed to slip the piece of metal between 2 bits of rubber on one of his clogs."

"What a marvellous man!" I exclaimed.

"There's better than that," Espadon went on. "I went to see him and told him that it was absolutely essential that the Germans should not know that we had a piece of the metal. He went on with his work at the factory and never told a soul. None of his companions would speak to him now after that business on 11 November; they treated him as a pariah and avoided him like the plague. They looked on him as a traitor."

Bomber Offensive

As yet unable to mount the second front the Russians increasingly agitated for, the Allies tried to relieve Nazi pressure on the Eastern front by a stepped-up aerial offensive against Germany. The Royal Air Force had made sporadic raids against Germany in 1940 and 1941, but by 1942 the RAF Bomber Command was systematically battering German war industry. The big Halifax and Lancaster bombers roared into the night skies to drop their high-explosives and incendiaries on the Reich's major cities: Berlin, Lübeck, Rostock, Kiel, Karlsruhe, Stuttgart, Emden, Bremen, Duisburg, Hamburg, Mainz, Düsseldorf. On May 30, 1942, the RAF lashed at Cologne in the first 1000-plane raid of the war, and in June repeated the 1000-plane dose of devastation on the Ruhr and Bremen. Coventry and the London blitz were being avenged.

In Spring 1942 the American 8th Air Force was organized in England and its B-17 Flying Fortresses struck their first blows on August 18 against Rouen

A 12,000-pound bomb about to be loaded into a British Lancaster bomber. (Below) Lancasters about to go out on a night raid. The British pioneered the 1000-plane raids.

RAF was in favor of night bombing, but the Americans preferred day attacks.

and on October 8 against Lille. Though both air forces agreed strategically on the important targets: airplane factories, synthetic and natural oil installations, transport and communications networks, the Luftwaffe itself, and all the other essential war production of the Third Reich, they disagreed on tactics. The RAF favored night raids of saturation bombing; the 8th Air Force preferred day raids of precision bombing. Since the RAF bore the overwhelming burden of the aerial offensive during 1942, most of the raids were area-saturation night bombings. Those day raids flown suffered terrible, almost prohibitive losses because the Allies had not yet developed fighters with long enough

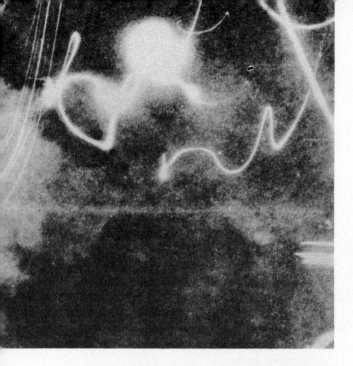

(Above) A British Lancaster over Hamburg surrounded by tracers from Nazi anti-aircraft fire. (Below) A Flying Fortress goes down, its wing buckled and blazing from flak.

More than half of Darmstadt, Germany, was destroyed by Allied bombers.

range to protect the bombers, and so day raids were kept at a minimum.

Göring's 1939 boast that if Berlin should ever be bombed, the German people could call him Meyer was now given its comeuppance. Neither Göring nor his Luftwaffe could halt the widening devastation of Allied bombing, and the 1000-plane raids were only an augury of the clouds of bombers to come.

Commando Raids

To relieve pressure on the Russians still further, the Allies launched a series of commando raids on the coast of Nazi-occupied Europe. In March 1941, British commandos hit the Lofoten Islands off the northwest coast of Norway and in December they raided Vaagso in Norway proper, blowing up installations, sinking shipping and bringing back prisoners and information. The big raids came in 1942 as diversionary efforts for the Red Army, but also to test the defenses of Hitler's Festung Europa and to stage dress rehearsals for the eventual assault on Europe which was to be the second front. In February, British commandos and paratroopers seized a German radar and radio station at Bruneval, in France, and brought back important devices and equipment. In March, British commandos and naval units drove the destroyer Campbeltown racing into St. Nazaire, the only port on the Atlantic coast that could hold the giant German battleship Tirpitz, and blew the drydock to smithereens. An anonymous commando participant recorded the accomplishment:

For the last few minutes before we landed, almost the whole convoy was floodlit. The coastal batteries began to bracket us. Shells were rustling overhead and plopping into the water. Many shells and machine-

gun bullets went straight through the ships, from side to side, killing men assembled below deck. We could see the docks now, our objective, and we could see the outline of jetties and warehouses which we had memorized day after day from maps and air photographs. All of us knew the place by heart. The Campbeltown changed course for the last time, and I saw her turn towards the dry dock.

This was the big moment. She put on speed. She was flying the White Ensign as she went in! She opened up with everything she had and charged the boom and the huge dock gates at eighteen knots, head on, with a German battery blazing at point-blank range across her decks. The troops were lying down, firing back with their Brens; the deck was stripped and they hadn't much cover. There was a mass of flame and smoke and gunfire. She went slap into the dock gates, we saw it happen, and lay there dead center. The gates were 35 feet thick and the Campbeltown went in with such power that she didn't stick till her bridge was level with them. The Tirpitz would think twice now about coming out into the Atlantic to attack our convoys. The Battle of the Atlantic wasn't going too well for the Allies then, and we had been told that our attack on St. Nazaire was not just a raid but an important part of Allied strategy. The destroyer had done her job. She crashed the dock at 1:33 A.M., that was 3 minutes after the time laid down in our orders. At 1:45 the troops were off. At 1:50 the scuttling charges were set off. At 2 o'clock she was abandoned and seen to be sinking. The 5 tons of explosive was concreted in and due to go off some hours later. The troops poured over the sides and knocked out the coastal battery alongside the dock. Another party blew up the pumping station and the station operating the dock gate. There were many wounded on board the doomed Campbeltown, and we got them all ashore. . . .

Most of us on shore were caught in the morning hiding in cellars and boiler rooms, waiting for a chance to get away next night. About 10:30 in the morning we heard the hell of an explosion. The Germans panicked, windows all over the town were smashed, and a huge pillar of flame shot up from the dry dock. The explosive in the Campeltown had gone off, and the huge dock gates and the 2 merchant ships inside had gone for 6. So that was that. It was no good for a year after at least. Some Germans were nosing about aboard the destroyer the moment she went up and went up with her. We were told that some of our lads had taken them aboard, but we never knew which of them had done this. I suppose we shall never know their names.

The largest "combined operation" was carried out by the Canadian 2nd Division and British commando units on August 19, 1942, a raid in force on Dieppe. The gains in experience of amphibious assault were bought at a bitter price, as were the Nazi units subsequently diverted from the thrust toward Stalingrad. Ross Munro, Canadian war correspondent, was on the bloody beaches of Dieppe:

The men in our boat crouched low, their faces tense and grim. They were awed by this unexpected blast of German fire, and it was their initiation to frightful battle noises. They gripped their weapons more tightly and waited for the ramp of our craft to go down.

We bumped on the beach and down went the ramp and out poured the first infantrymen. They plunged into about 2 feet of water and machine-gun bullets laced into them. Bodies piled up on the ramp. Some staggered to the beach and fell. Bullets were splatter-

In its first test at Dieppe, this tank landing barge was captured by Nazis.

ing into the boat itself, wounding and killing our men.

I was near the stern and to one side. Looking out the open bow over the bodies on the ramp, I saw the slope leading a short way up to a stone wall littered with Royals casualties. There must have been 60 or 70 of them, lying sprawled on the green grass and the brown earth. They had been cut down before they had a chance to fire a shot.

A dozen Canadians were running along the edge of the cliff toward the stone wall. They carried their weapons and some were firing as they ran. But some had no helmets, some were already wounded, their uniforms torn and bloody. One by one they were cut down and rolled down the slope to the sea.

I don't know how long we were nosed down on that beach. It may have been five minutes. It may have been 20. On no other front have I witnessed such a

Canadian commandos carry their wounded as their Nazi captors stand by.

carnage. It was brutal and terrible and shocked you almost to insensibility to see the piles of dead and feel the hopelessness of the attack at this point.

There was one young lad crouching 6 feet away from me. He had made several vain attempts to rush down the ramp to the beach but each time a hail of fire had driven him back. He had been wounded in the arm but was determined to try again. He lunged forward and a streak of red-white tracer slashed through his stomach.

I'll never forget his anguished cry as he collapsed on the blood-soaked deck: "Christ, we gotta beat them; we gotta beat them!" He was dead in a few minutes.

The Canadians learned the hard way that Hitler's Fortress Europe was heavily fortified and skillfully defended, and their casualties were brutally high. Of 4963 men who hit the Dieppe beaches, less than half —2211— returned, almost 2000 were taken prisoner,

69

An Allied freighter burns after being attacked by long-range Nazi bombers.

and almost 1,000 wounded. Though this bloody foray did not persuade Stalin that a second front was not immediately possible, it did convince the Allies.

The Battle of the Atlantic

"The Battle of the Atlantic was the dominating factor all through the war," Winston Churchill stated. On winning that battle depended not only British and Soviet survival, but ultimate Allied victory over the Axis. The struggle for the Atlantic lifeline reached its peak during the first six months of 1942. U-boats struck with impunity all along the American eastern seaboard, from Brazil to Newfoundland, sinking more than 3,000,-000 tons of merchant shipping in that catastrophic half-year. They concentrated on the oil tankers which ran from Venezuela and Mexico to New Orleans and United States East Coast ports, to stop the flow of the precious fluid that fueled and lubricated the engines of war.

Though courage and perseverance played their essential roles, the war at sea increasingly became one of production, science, and tactics. America performed shipbuilding prodigies. In the crucial year 1942, the U.S. turned out 8,000,000 gross tons of all types of shipping, and in 1943 boosted it to 20,000,000 tons. Combined Allied construction of merchant shipping alone more than doubled between 1942 and 1943, from 7,000,000 to more than 14,500,000 gross tons, outstripping losses by almost 11,000,000 gross tons.

But building more ships was only one part of the Allied program; the other was reducing the number of ships sunk. Menaced by magnetic mines and acoustical torpedoes, Allied scientists produced counterdevices to neutralize them. Attacked by U-boats, sur-

face raiders, and aircraft, Allied navies and air forces worked out new detection devices—sonar and radar—and guarded their shipping with a convoy and patrol system. German Grand Admiral Karl Doenitz sent "wolf-packs" of submarines to prey on Allied ships. Strung out along a convoy route, they wearied the defenses by attacking day after day for long periods of time. To keep them at sea longer, Doenitz sent surface ships to supply and refuel them. The Allies countered with more destroyers, corvettes, and escort aircraft carriers—the "baby flat-tops"—to locate and destroy the wolf-packs. A series of air bases were also established in Labrador, Newfoundland, Greenland, and Iceland from which long-range land-based bombers added their continuous air cover to North Atlantic convoys. In addition, these bases permitted heavy bombers to fly across the Atlantic in several shorter hops, saving

(Left) An American Coast Guardsman dead by his smashed 40-mm ack-ack gun after a German air attack. (Below) A seamen off a stricken ship is helped by a rescue team.

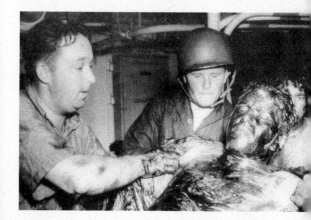

The crew of a Coast Guard cutter watches as a pattern of depth charges explodes in the North Atlantic. (Below) A Nazi submarine about to sink after being forced to surface by depth charges and then hit with gunfire.

shipping and assembling, and speeding the build-up of Allied air power in Britain.

In spite of Allied bombing of submarine factories and U-boat pens, and losses at sea, Admiral Doenitz was able to put increasing numbers of his "pig boats" into operation, with greater range and striking power, because German production concentrated on its efficient production of submarines. The Schnorkel breathing device, developed late in the war, even allowed German U boats to remain underwater almost all the time they were at sea.

But try as they would, the Nazis were no match for Allied resources. During the course of the entire war the Allies lost 23,500,000 gross tons of merchant shipping and built 45,600,000 gross tons to replace it. More than 14,000,000 tons of what was lost was sent to the bottom by U boats, but sinkings declined and construction soared, and the Allies destroyed 781 German submarines. Though the Allies could never relax their vigilance, by the end of 1943, the crisis was over, and they had won the Battle of the Atlantic.

The Murmansk Run

With Nazi spearheads deep in Russia, the Western Allies strained to send planes, tanks, and guns to help the Soviets fend them off. These had to go by ship and only three routes were available. Across the North Atlantic to Murmansk and Archangel was the shortest, fastest, and most dangerous. Around the Cape of Good Hope to Iran and up the Trans-Iranian Railway into southern Russia was much safer, but also much slower. Across the Pacific from the American West Coast to Siberia, a route controlled in large measure by the Japanese Navy, left cargo thousands of miles from the European fighting fronts and with only the overburdened and inadequate facilities of the Trans-Siberian Railway to transport it.

Nazi successes increased Russian agitation for a second front and for sending convoys on the shortest run. The first small convoys to Murmansk had been sent from Britain only a month after the Nazis invaded Russia and by February 1942 the convoys were of considerable size. To stop that flow of supplies, Hitler concentrated planes, submarines, and most of his heavy naval units in Norway. With periods of almost perpetual daylight affording no concealment and the northern pack ice an added hazard, the Allies and Britain particularly suffered cruel losses in trying to push the Arctic convoys through. Robert Carse gives some of the flavor of a British convoy to Murmansk on which he sailed:

The snow and the sleet squalls passed. Wednesday gave a clear cerulean sky, a blue and gleaming sea, very little horizon or zenith cloud. This was their day, the Nazis', we knew. We dragged our ammunition cases closer to the guns; got ready as well as we could.

They came early: the Heinkels, the Messerschmitts, the Stukas, the Junkers 89's, and all told there were 105 of them over us during that day's fight that was to last 20 hours. They used everything: 1100-pounders, 550's, 250's, aerial torpedoes, mines, their cannons, and their machine guns; while outside, always trying to get in, their submarines rushed our escort.

That was hell. There is no other word I know for it. Everywhere you looked aloft you saw them, crossing and recrossing us, hammering down and back, the bombs brown, sleek in the air, screaming to burst furiously white in the sea. All around us, as so slowly we kept on going, the pure blue of the sea was mottled

76

Planes working from light carriers were deadly against Nazi submarines.

blackish with the greasy patches of their bomb discharges. Our ship was missed closely time and again. We drew our breaths in a kind of gasping choke. . . .

The aftermost plane peeled off, banking towards the ship astern. The other kept on, right into our fire, smack for us. Then he dropped it, a 550-pounder. He was gone, away from our fire, and, hanging to the guns, all we could do was look up at that bomb.

It fell, slanting with the pull of the plane's speed. It whirled, screaming and howling in the air directly overhead. We could very clearly see the cylindrical khaki shape, the fins, even the white blur that was the serial markings on the side. This was for us, we thought. This was death. Even if it should miss, the concussion will take the TNT [the ship's cargo].

There was nothing to do but hang on tighter to the gun grips. We said good-by to each other, but the bomb held our ears, the sound of it seemed to possess all sound.

Then in some sudden and not-yet-strong gust of wind it veered a bit. It struck the sea no more than twenty-five feet astern of us. There was the impact of passage into the sea, an immense, rushing smack, then the detonation. My wife's image was before my eyes. I stood there waiting for the TNT.

Water went tumbling over me in a dousing, blinding column. The ship rose and fell, groaning, terribly shaking. Empty cartridges jumped under the shock, pitched off into the sea. Beneath my feet, as the ship still jarred from that awful violence, the deck seams opened, and the oakum lay loose. . . .

The ship was still going on, although now there was a great, grinding thump from the propeller under us. We were in a bad way, we knew. We had been damaged plenty below.

The Chief, quiet and bespectacled, came aft to look at her and told us that 9 of the 10 main bearings on the shaft had been shattered. There was a bad twist in the tail-shaft itself, and plates had been stove in the shaft alleyway. She was taking water there, but, for the time being, the pumps could handle that. We kept on going up to Russia.

The sacrifices on the Murmansk run helped the Red armies stave off defeat early in the war, and later to turn to the offensive. By spring of 1942, three-fourths of British munitions production was going to the USSR and total deliveries to the Russians were of unprecedented scope. Though nothing could repay Russia for its losses in blood, the Allies did not stint and thereby they helped the Soviet weather the storm.

The Channel Dash

Hitler was obsessed with the idea that the Allies would first invade Norway. That, obstructing the Murmansk convoys, and keeping the British Home Fleet pinned down, made him concentrate his heaviest surface raiders in Norwegian waters. But 3 of his best big ships were at Brest, on the French coast, and continually under the eyes and bombs of the RAF. On the night of February 11, 1942, the battlecruisers Scharnhorst and Gneisenau and the 8-inch cruiser Prinz Eugen left Brest and raced north for their home bases. Taking advantage of fog and a new, intensified German jamming of British radar, and protected by destroyers and a constant Luftwaffe umbrella, the German ships dashed around Brittany. Moving swiftly past the heavy guns of British shore batteries at Dover, the ships managed to reach the Belgian coast before they were discovered, just before noon the next day. Immedi-

An aerial view of the Tirpitz in the fjord where it was sunk by RAF bombers.

ately, the British threw bombers and torpedo planes, destroyers and motor torpedo boats, into the attack on them, but the German ships beat off their attackers and got through to their home ports. But not quite unscathed; the Scharnhorst and Gneisenau had both been damaged by mines.

Thereafter the Royal Navy and the RAF gave them no peace. That same month the RAF bombed the Scharnhorst at Wilhelmshaven and the Gneisenau at Kiel. The latter never recovered from the mine damage and never again poked its nose out during the war. A British submarine, the Trident, torpedoed the Prinz Eugen and forced it to tie up at Trondheim. The next month, March 1942, the 42,000-ton super-battleship Tirpitz, sister ship of the Bismarck, sallied forth to strike a Murmansk convoy. It was caught and driven back to West Fjord by the British battleship King George V and the carrier Victorious.

In September 1943, both the Tirpitz and Scharnhorst, with an escort of 10 destroyers, raided Allied installations on Spitzbergen and wrought havoc there. On Christmas Day, the Scharnhorst put out again to slash at a Murmansk convoy, but this time it was caught. Engaged by the convoy's escort of three British cruisers, its 11-inch guns damaged the Norfolk, and was in turn hurt by the Norfolk's 8-inch guns. The battleship Duke of York, with Home Fleet commander Admiral Sir Bruce Fraser aboard, raced up and his 14-inch guns smashed the Scharnhorst to a halt. His escort cruiser Jamaica then sent the German battle-cruiser to the bottom with a salvo of torpedoes. The Tirpitz, after being hit by everything from bombers to midget submarines, finally succumbed in November 1944 when RAF Lancasters hit it in Tromso Fjord. For all practical purposes, the German Navy had been neutralized.

The Counteroffensives

Guadalcanal and New Guinea

In spring 1942 the Battle of Midway had halted the Japanese thrust into the Central Pacific and the Battle of Coral Sea frustrated their assault on Port Moresby in New Guinea. That summer the Japanese grimly continued to try to expand their outer defense ring by dividing their forces into a pincers reaching down both sides of the Coral Sea, the right wing toward Port Moresby once more, the left into the southern Solomon Islands. As part of their Coral Sea expedition, the Japanese had already taken the fine harbor at Tulagi and they now began to build an airfield on Guadalcanal across the channel from it. Success might give air and naval mastery of the Coral Sea, sever the American supply line to Australia, and menace northeastern Australia and the newly occupied American bases on New Caledonia and in the New Hebrides.

But if the Japanese could send two pincers south, so the Allies, if they defeated the Japanese assault, could send them north. Control of New Guinea and the Solomons would permit the Allies to outflank and cut off Rabaul and Kavieng, Japan's major Southwest Pacifc bases along the "Bismarck barrier."

Although the battles for New Guinea and Guadalcanal were fought under separate Allied commanders—New Guinea under General Douglas MacArthur's Southwest Pacific Area command and Guadalcanal under Admiral Chester Nimitz's Pacific Ocean Area—they were part and parcel of the same campaign on opposite fringes of the Coral Sea. And the Japanese strategy, and perhaps necessity, to divide their forces between the two battles may have cost them victory in both.

Out of the tropical, disease-ridden New Guinea jungles towers the 13,000-foot mountainous backbone

During the summer of 1942, Japanese forces held grimly to the offensive in New Guinea. Fierce-fighting Australians (above) assisted by natives (below) managed to hold and even eliminate a Japanese force at Milne Bay.

MacArthur, who commanded the assault on New Guinea.

of the island, the Owen Stanley Range, natural defense line of the Allied bastion at Port Moresby. From their Lae and Salamaua bases on New Guinea's north coast, the Japanese tried simultaneously to pierce and outflank the Owen Stanleys which separated them from Port Moresby on the south coast. In a series of amphibious landings in early July they took Buna and Gona, halfway between Lae and Milne Bay at the southeast tip of the island. From there, late in July, one Japanese spearhead drove overland along the narrow Kokoda Trail which led through a 6700-foot high gap in the mountains and down toward Port Moresby. On August 26, the other spearhead, an amphibious assault by Japanese marines, landed near Milne Bay. If the Japanese took Milne Bay and the three new airstrips MacArthur was building there, they could outflank the Owen Stanleys and take Port Moresby. The Milne Bay

An Army mortar team firing during the drive toward Buna.

airstrips, combined with the Guadalcanal air base, assured them mastery of the skies over the Coral Sea.

In spite of fierce Australian rear-guard fighting the Japanese reached Kokoda Village on August 3 and by the end of September were only 32 miles from Port Moresby. Here, at the village of Ioribaiwa, worn out by combat, starvation and disease, hurt by American air attacks on their communications and forward columns, the Japanese offensive limped to a halt, and the Australians counterattacked.

Meanwhile, the Japanese marines at Milne Bay were cut to ribbons by the Australians, and were forced to evacuate their beachhead after 10 days of bitter fighting. By the second week in September the Japanese Navy had taken them off the beaches, but they left all their heavy equipment, considerable supplies, and half their number dead behind them.

The Australian counterattack on the Kokoda Trail moved painfully forward. How they endured the "mosquitos, mud, mountains, malaria and monotony," not to speak of driving the tenacious Japanese back across the Owen Stanleys, is recounted by George H. Johnston, who called it "the toughest fighting in the world":

On the Kokoda track, however, after you've been walking a few hours, you soon get above the mosquito country. As the troops toiled and grunted up they would often stop and gasp with amazement at the enormous butterflies that drifted to and fro, or alighted on their arms to drink the sweat. The insect life, from scorpions to butterflies, is impressive.

Only for a time though. You eventually reach a stage when flora and fauna, and even the Japs, gradually lose interest. Your mental processes allow you to be conscious of only one thing—"The Track," or, more casually, "The Bloody Track." You listen to your legs creaking and stare at the ground and think of the next stretch of mud, and you wonder if the hills will ever end. Up one almost perpendicular mountain face more than 2000 steps have been cut out of the mud and built up with felled saplings inside which the packed earth has long since become black glue. Each step is two feet high. You slip on one in three. There are no resting places. Climbing it is the supreme agony of mind and spirit. The troops, with fine irony, have christened it "The Golden Staircase."

Life changes as you push up the track. Standards of living deteriorate, sometimes below normally accepted standards even of primitive existence. Thoughts become somber, humor takes on a grim, almost macabre quality. When men reach the nadir of mental and physical agony there are times when sickness or injury or even death seem like things to be welcomed. Near

An Army patrol searching for the enemy along the banks of the Giruwa River in New Guinea. The men shown had volunteered and were awarded Distinguished Service Crosses.

Efogi, on a slimy section of the track that reeks with the stench of death, the remains of an enemy soldier lie on a crude stretcher, abandoned by the Japanese retreat. The flesh has gone from his bones, and a white, bony claw sticks out of a ragged uniform sleeve, stretching across the track. Every Australian who passes, plodding up the muddy rise that leads to the pass, grasps the skeleton's grisly hand, shakes it fervently and says "Good on you, sport!" before moving wearily on.

In this territory the Japanese are fighting, with a stubborn tenacity that is almost unbelievable, from an elaborate system of prepared positions along every ridge and spur. Churned up by the troops of both armies, the track itself is knee deep in thick, black mud. For the last 10 days no man's clothing has been dry and they have slept — when sleep was possible — in pouring rain under sodden blankets. Each man carries all his personal equipment, firearms, ammunition supply and 5 days' rations. Every hour is a nightmare.

On November 2, the Australians entered abandoned Kokoda Village, pushed across the rest of the Owen Stanleys and pursued the fleeing Japanese into the swamps and kunai grass around Gona and Buna. On November 16, in a daring maneuver, MacArthur airlifted 15,000 Americans to a point 7 miles south of Buna, and overland Australians and airborne Americans together assaulted the Japanese coastal footholds there. In savage fighting, they penned the defending Japanese into an ever narrowing strip of beach and jungle until on December 10, they stormed Gona, on January 3, 1943, Buna, and on January 23 finished the campaign by annihilating the stubborn remnants of the Japanese forces on Sanananda Point.

Forced to choose between holding Guadalcanal or their New Guinea bases, the Japanese chose New Guinea and moved swiftly to strengthen their positions at Lae and Salamaua. On March 3–4, 1943, however, B-17s, B-25s, A-20s, and P-38s from General George C. Kenney's Southwest Pacific Air Command caught a huge Japanese convoy in the Bismarck Sea ferrying troops from Rabaul to Lae. Though the extent of the damage inflicted on the Japanese convoy has been disputed, there is little doubt that Japanese plans suffered a severe setback. The minimum damage to the Japanese was probably 12 ships sunk, more than 30 planes shot down, and 3000 Japanese troops wiped out; the maximum damage is estimated as many more ships and planes and several divisions of Japanese troops. In the battle, the United States lost only four planes.

The campaign in Papua, Australian New Guinea, was over, but its victories had been bought with almost 16,000 American and Australian casualties. The rest of New Guinea was still to come.

"Operation Cactus"

In July, at about the same time as the Japanese advance began in New Guinea, Australian "coastwatchers" and U.S. reconnaissance planes reported that the Japanese airfield on Guadalcanal would be completed before the end of August. The American First Marine Division, under the command of Major General Alexander A. Vandegrift, was hastily embarked from New Zealand and set sail in a task force under over-all command of Vice-Admiral Robert L. Ghormley. On August 7 they invaded Guadalcanal and its neighboring islands — Tulagi, Gavutu, and Tanambogo. Within two days the 18,000 Marines and Raiders had taken three of the four islands and set off six months of ground, sea and air combat on the fourth, in what was to be one of the longest and most bitterly contested campaigns in the Pacific war.

Appropriately the Guadalcanal operation was given the code name "Cactus" and no fighting was thornier. As in New Guinea, not only were the Americans fighting a tenacious and determined enemy, but geography as well. The Solomon Islands are a volcanic archipelago of 7 big islands and 10 small ones which stretches in two parallel chains from northwest to southeast, 600 miles from Buka at the northwestern tip of the chain to San Cristobal at the southeastern end. Guadalcanal is next to the last island in the southeast chain. Mountainous, slashed by gullies and ravines, covered with teeming equatorial jungles and plains with kunai grass higher than a man's head, Guadalcanal's steaming wet climate is the breeding ground of malaria, dengue, typhus, dysentery, and a host of other tropical diseases.

Geography also gave the Japanese a strategic advantage. Their neighboring bases at Rabaul and Kavieng in the Bismarck Archipelago, and their huge naval installations at Truk in the Carolines, were reinforced by advanced air and naval bases in the northern Solomons — Buin, the Shortlands Islands, Rekata Bay — and gave them an advantage in the fight for sea and air superiority around Guadalcanal.

The focus of the campaign was, therefore, the vital Japanese airfield on Guadalcanal, renamed Henderson Field by the Americans after Major Lofton R. Henderson, the Marine Corps pilot killed in attacking the Japanese carriers at Midway. The Marines took the still uncompleted airfield on the second day after the landing. If they were to survive, they had to hold it to seize command of the air over the island. Though the landings had been effected with little Japanese resistance, the enemy now reacted swiftly and savagely.

Early on the morning of August 9, Japanese Admiral Gunichi Mikawa led a task force of 5 heavy cruisers, 2 light ones, and a destroyer down "The Slot" — the channel that separated the twin strands of the Solomon archipelago — to strike at the landings. In a night battle off Savo Island, the Japanese smashed an Allied naval squadron guarding the landings, sinking 4 cruisers, one of them Australian, and heavily damaging another. But, inexplicably, Mikawa withdrew his ships before daylight without striking at the now unprotected transports and beaches. The following day the transports, still half unloaded, and the task force's carrier air cover, pulled out and left the Marines to their own courageous devices.

An American destroyer in action during the battles for the Solomons.

From there on the Marines had their work cut out for them. On an island 90 miles long and 25 miles wide, they held a perimeter 7 miles long and 4 miles wide around prized Henderson Field. In a few days they had finished the airfield and made it operational. The problem now was who could pour supplies and replacements into Guadalcanal more quickly. At first the Japanese had command of both sea and air, but as soon as planes were able to fly from Henderson the situation gradually changed. During the day Marine dive bombers and fighters and Army Flying Fortresses dominated the skies and waters around Guadalcanal, but at night the Japanese were the masters. During the day, therefore, the Americans were able to put troops and materials ashore with few losses. The Japanese, on the other hand, kept trying to reinforce their positions at night. The wily and skillful Rear Admiral Raizo Tanaka sent his "Tokyo Express"—a task force of destroyers and transports—down "The Slot" between Santa Isabel and New Georgia islands to raid and harass the Americans and to reinforce the Japanese troops ashore and replenish their supplies. But in the early mornings American bombers frequently caught and sank Tanaka's ships as they raced back toward their bases, and destroyed enemy troops and supplies still on the beaches.

But Henderson Field remained the key. If the Japanese captured it or knocked it out, they could then risk a major amphibious assault to drive the Marines into the Coral Sea. Shelled by everything from battleships to submarines, bombed from the air, bombarded by artillery and mortars, the Marines grimly held on to Henderson in bitter ground fighting. Often the Japanese seemed only an ace away from taking the field, or knocking out its planes, fuel dumps, repair depots, and landing strips, but they never quite succeeded.

The determined Japanese tried on sea, on the ground, and in the air. In the prolonged battle between August 1942 and January 1943, six major naval engagements were fought in the waters adjacent to the island. So many ships were sunk that Marines began to call the waters around Savo Island "Iron Bottom Bay" because it was littered with the hulks of sunken ships. In battles that were to take their place in U.S. naval history—Savo Island, Eastern Solomons, Cape Esperance, Santa Cruz Islands, Guadalcanal, and Tassafaronga—both sides suffered heavy losses in men and ships. Almost all were fought to prevent or to implement troop and supply landings. The United States lost 24 ships in those encounters: 2 aircraft carriers (the Wasp and the Hornet), 6 heavy cruisers, 2 light cruisers, and 14 destroyers. The Japanese also lost 24 war ships: 2 battleships, 1 light aircraft carrier, 3 heavy cruisers, 1 light cruiser, 11 destroyers, and 6 submarines. Many other naval units on both sides—carriers, battleships, and cruisers—were heavily damaged and put out of action for long periods of time.

Ferocious air battles were fought to gain control over the island. But neither the Buin airfield at Bougainville, nor their new air strip at Munda Point on New Georgia Island, could provide adequate fighter cover for Japanese naval vessels, troop transports, or bombers. Marine planes shot the Japanese escorting fighters out of the sky and bombers smashed at convoys, air bases, and war ships, and kept Henderson from being put out of commission.

In the bitter ground fighting, in battles whose strange names were also to go down in Marine annals, such as Tenaru River, Bloody Ridge, Matanikau River, Henderson Field, Point Cruz, the Gifu, Galloping Horse, the

The landings on Guadalcanal were made against only light resistance, but the

Japanese soon began to fight back bitterly against the First Marine Division.

The Japanese assault used artillery, planes and a naval bombardment.

Marines held and inflicted bloody losses on the Japanese.

In the fiercely contested Battle of Tenaru River, Robert Leckie, who fought there, tells how the fighting went:

Dawn seemed to burst from a mortar tube. The two coincided; the rising bombardment of our mortars and the arrival of light. We could see, now, that the coconut grove directly opposite us had no life in it. There were bodies, but no living enemy.

But to the left, toward the ocean and across the Tenaru, the remnant of this defeated Japanese attacking force was being annihilated. We could see them, running. Our mortars had got behind them. We were walking our fire in; that is, dropping shells to the enemy's rear, then lobbing the projectiles steadily closer to our own lines, so that the unfortunate foe was forced to abandon cover after cover, being drawn inexorably toward our front, where he was at last flushed and destroyed.

We could see them flitting from tree to tree. The Gentleman's gun was in an excellent position to enfilade. He did. He fired long bursts at them. Some of us fired our rifles. But we were out of the fight, now; way off on the extreme right flank. We could add nothing to a situation so obviously under control. . . .

Infantry had crossed the Tenaru at the bridge to our right and were fanning out in the coconut grove. They would sweep toward the ocean.

Light tanks were crossing the sandspit far to the left, leading a counterattack.

The Japanese were being nailed into a coffin. . . .

Men of the 1st Battalion were cleaning up. Sometimes they drove a Japanese toward us. He would cower on the river bank, hiding: unaware that opposite him were we, already the victors, numerous, heavily armed, lusting for more blood. We killed a few more this way. The Fever was on us.

Down on the sandspit the last nail was being driven into the coffin.

Some of the Japanese threw themselves into the channel and swam away from that grove of horror. They were like lemmings. They could not come back. Their heads bobbed like corks on the horizon. The Marines killed them from the prone position; the Marines lay on their bellies in the sand and shot them through the head.

The battle was over.

Not only the fighting on Guadalcanal was terrifying. Waiting in the dark jungles—on land, too, the Japanese most often made their attacks at night—was also terrifying, and Marine Leckie describes it:

Our entrenching tools made muffled noises while we scooped foxholes out of the jungle floor. It was like digging into a compost heap ten thousand years old. Beneath this perfection of corruption lay a dark rich loam. We had barely finished when night fell, abruptly, blackly, like a shade drawn swiftly down from jungle room to jungle floor. We slipped into the foxholes. We lay down and waited.

It was a darkness without time. It was an impenetrable darkness. To the right and left of me rose up those terrible formless things of my imagination, which I could not see because there was no light. I could not see, but I dared not close my eyes lest the darkness crawl beneath my eyelids and suffocate me. I could only hear. My ears became my being and I could hear the specks of life that crawled beneath my clothing, the rotting of the great tree which rose from its three-cornered trunk above me. I could hear the darknesses

Fires burn on Guadalcanal (left) as Marine artillery (below) fought to hold on to the all-important airstrip, Henderson Field. Capture of the field would have given the enemy air control over and around the island. Although some Japanese prisoners (above) were taken, most fought until they fell.

gathering against me and the silences that lay between the moving things.

I could hear the enemy everywhere about me, whispering to each other and calling my name. I lay openmouthed and half-mad beneath that giant tree. I had not looked into its foliage before the darkness and now I fancied it infested with Japanese. Everything and all the world became my enemy, and soon my very body betrayed me and became my foe. My leg became a sleeping Japanese, and then the other leg. My arms, too, and then my head.

My heart was alone. It was me. I was my heart.

It lay quivering. I lay quivering, in that rotten hole while the darkness gathered and all creation conspired for my heart.

How long? I lay for an eternity. There was no time. Time had disintegrated in that black void. There was only emptiness, and that is something; there was only being; there was only consciousness.

Like the light that comes up suddenly in a darkened theatre, daylight came quickly. Dawn came, and so myself came back to myself. I could see the pale outlines of my comrades to right and left, and I marveled to see how tame my tree could be, how unforbidding could be its branches.

I know now why men light fires.

By the end of 1942, reinforced on the ground by Army troops, and in the air, and with new commanders —Admiral William F. "Bull" Halsey replacing Ghormley as Task Force Commander, and Army Major General Alexander M. Patch as ground commander—the Marines and Army forces went over to the offensive to drive the Japanese off the island. The Allied thrust in New Guinea now so menaced Japanese positions there that the Japanese were forced to divert the 50,000 troops they had massed at Rabaul for an all-out assault on Guadalcanal to defend their New Guinea bases.

The Japanese now had to surrender or die. Some chose to fight to the death. Others made suicidal Banzai charges singing the hymn to the Emperor, only to be cut down like chaff by Marine and Army fire. But many were able to escape. In a brilliant operation, Admiral Tanaka again sent his "Tokyo Express" down "The Slot" for the last times and on three nights, from February 7, 1943 to February 9, re-embarked 16,000 Japanese troops from Cape Esperance.

The battle was over; Guadalcanal was secured.

To hold the island the Japanese had lost almost 50,000 men, killed, wounded and drowned in transit, and many to hunger and disease as well. The Americans had only 4000 killed and wounded, but the suffering could not be measured by casualties alone. As Robert Leckie tells it, the best summary of Guadalcanal was what he saw on a Marine's grave there:

And when he gets to Heaven
To St. Peter he will tell:
One more Marine reporting, sir—
I've served my time in Hell.

El Alamein

During the late summer and early fall of 1942, the Allies and the Axis once more fought the crucial war of reinforcement in the desert. Axis troops were still only 60 miles from Alexandria and as late as October, Rommel asserted:

We hold the gateway of Egypt with full intention to act. We did not go there with any intention of being flung back sooner or later. You may rely on our holding fast to what we have got.

But with the Germans deeply committed on the Russian front the seesaw battle of supply in Africa had finally and permanently shifted in favor of the Allies. General Bernard Montgomery, new Eighth Army commander, confidently promised:

Give me a fortnight and I can resist the German attack. Give me three weeks, and I can defeat the Boche. Give me a month, and I can chase him out of Africa.

He was soon to fulfill his promise.

British and American supplies together had given Montgomery a decided edge over his rival in tanks, guns, planes, transport, and men. He now had 1000 tanks to fewer than 600 for Rommel, a 2–1 advantage in planes, and overpowering superiority in artillery. Moreover, the quality of his equipment was now, for the first time, equal to or better than Rommel's. With its back to the Delta, the Eighth Army was operating on short supply lines and the RAF and Royal Navy were slashing Rommel's extended sea and overland lines of supply to shreds. Three-quarters of his seaborne supplies were sunk en route along with more than 200,000 tons of Axis shipping. As a result, of the 30,000 tons of supplies he needed every month, Rommel was getting only a fifth, or 6000 tons. He was short of fuel, ammunition and water.

On October 23, after an intense 800-gun artillery bombardment, Montgomery opened his attack. Rommel's lines were protected by defenses in depth, with what Rommel called "Devil's Gardens" of minefields, barbed wire and fields of murderous cross-fire. At Alamein there was no room for flanking maneuver: the defenses had to be broken. After 12 days of bitter fighting and 13,000 casualties, Montgomery pierced the Axis positions and sent his armor plunging through the gaps. In a sensitive portrayal of the fighting, H. P. Samwell, then a lieutenant in the Argyll and Sutherland Highlanders, describes what leading a platoon into the attack was like:

Oddly enough I don't remember the actual start— one moment I was lying on my stomach on the open rocky desert, the next I was walking steadily as if out for an evening stroll, on the right of a long line of men in extended order. . . .

I suddenly discovered that I was still carrying my ash

Part of the British, Indian, South African, Australian and New Zealand force which Montgomery led at El Alamein.

stick. I had meant to leave it at the rear Company H.Q. and exchange it for a rifle. I smiled to myself to think I was walking straight towards the enemy armed only with a .38 pistol and nine rounds of ammunition. Well, it was too late to do anything about it now, but I expected that someone would soon be hit and I could take his. I began to wonder, still quite impersonally, who it would be; perhaps myself! in which case I wouldn't need a rifle. Then I heard a new sound above the roar of the guns and the explosion of shells. The sharp rat-tat-tat of Breda and Spandau machine-guns — streams of tracer bullets whined diagonally across our front, not more than 20 yards ahead. We must be getting near the first enemy positions. I asked the pace-checker on my right how many paces we had done. He grinned and said he had lost count; then crump-crump-crump! a new sharper note. This was something that

The crew of a knocked-out German tank surrenders to the onrushing

affected us—mortar shells were landing right among us. I heard a man on my left say, "Oh, God!" and I saw him stagger and fall. The major was shouting again. I couldn't hear what he said, but his company seemed to be already at grips with the enemy. At that moment I saw a single strand of wire ahead about breast high. I took a running jump at it and just cleared it. My sergeant, coming behind, started to climb over it, and immediately there was a blinding flash and blast of air struck me on the back of the neck. I never saw that sergeant again. I remember wondering what instinct had made me jump that wire. Strange? I hadn't been thinking of booby-traps. We had broken into a run now —why, I don't know. Nobody had given any order. A corporal on my left was firing his Bren gun from the hip. I wondered if he was really firing at anything. Then suddenly I saw a head and shoulders protruding

British at El Alamein. Rommel led most of his Afrika Korps out of the trap.

from a hole in the ground. I had already passed it and had to turn half round. I fired my pistol three times, and then ran on to catch up the line.

The line had broken up into blobs of men struggling together; my faithful batman was still trotting along beside me. I wondered if he had been with me while I was shooting. My runner had disappeared, though; and then I saw some men in a trench ahead of me. They were standing up with their hands above their heads screaming something that sounded like "Mardray." I remember thinking how dirty and ill-fitting their uniforms were, and smiled at myself for bothering about that at this time. To my left and behind me some of the N.C.O.s were rounding up prisoners and kicking them into some sort of formation. I waved my pistol at the men in front with their hands up to sign them to join the others. In front of me a terrified Italian was running round and round with his hands above his head screaming at the top of his voice. The men I had signalled started to come out. Suddenly I heard a shout of "Watch out!" and the next moment something hard hit the toe of my boot and bounced off. There was a blinding explosion, and I staggered back holding my arm over my eyes instinctively. Was I wounded? I looked down rather expecting to see blood pouring out, but there was nothing—a tremendous feeling of relief. I was unhurt. I looked for the sergeant who had been beside me; he had come up to take the place of the one who had fallen. At first I couldn't see him, and then I saw him lying sprawled out on his back groaning. His leg was just a tangled mess. I realised all at once what had happened: one of enemy in the trench had thrown a grenade at me as he came out with his hands up. It had bounced off my boot as the sergeant shouted his warning, and had exploded beside him. I suddenly felt furious; an absolutely uncontrollable temper surged up inside me. I swore and cursed at the enemy now crouching in the corner of the trench; then I fired at them at point-blank range—one, two, three, and then click! I had forgotten to reload. I flung my pistol away in disgust and grabbed a rifle—the sergeant's, I think—and rushed in. I believe two of the enemy were sprawled on the ground at the bottom of the square trench. I bayoneted two more and then came out again. I was quite cool now, and I started looking for my pistol, and thinking to myself there will be hell to pay with the quartermaster if I can't account for it. The firing had died down and groups of men were collecting round me rather vaguely; just then a man shouted and fired a single round. I afterwards learnt that one of the enemy in the trench had heaved himself up and was just going to fire into my back when my man saw him and shot him first.

By November 4 the Axis troops were in headlong retreat. It was now a race to see if Montgomery could capture or annihilate Rommel's forces, or if the Desert Fox, who two days after the offensive began had flown back from a German hospital to resume command, could once again extricate his troops. Rommel mustered all his precious fuel to rescue his Afrika Korps and his best weapons. By ruthlessly jettisoning every nonessential—including his Italian infantry—he was able to elude capture and keep the retreat from turning into a rout.

This time, with losses numbering about 75,000 men, 1000 guns and 500 tanks, there was to be no Axis stand along the way for any length of time. In three months, and with miracles of coordination keeping his supplies flowing, Montgomery was to drive Rommel

1500 miles across the last remnants of Italy's African empire to Tunisia, though weather and the Desert Fox's skill once more combined in helping the Axis forces to elude annihilation. But only for a while, for on November 8, on the other side of Africa, Anglo-American forces had landed, and Rommel was caught between the hammer and the anvil.

"Torch": The End in Africa

On the night of November 8, while the battle still raged at Alamein, an 850-ship Anglo-American armada, whose parts had sailed separately from Britain and the U. S., launched coordinated assaults on the Atlantic and Mediterranean coasts of French North Africa. The immediate military targets were the Algerian ports of Oran and Algiers, and Casablanca in Morocco. Back of the landings were almost half a year of military and political preparations under the code name of "Torch."

German prisoners (left) stream to the rear while in the background a convoy

Everywhere, in conception and execution, the political impinged on the military in "Torch," and the problems of both were enormous, complex, and trying.

First, the North African invasion was a substitute for the cross-Channel assault on Europe which the Soviets were clamoring for, and for which the Allies did not yet have the necessary forces. With the Russians fighting for their lives at Stalingrad just then, "Torch" would at least provide a "limited second front" in Africa to divert the Axis. Second, if Rommel could be trapped between the pincers of the British Eighth Army moving west and the Anglo-American forces moving east, a resounding defeat would be inflicted on Axis troops and morale. Third, control of the Mediterranean coast would then provide a springboard for invading the "soft underbelly" of Europe and might force the Italians — who had little enough stomach for the war — to sue for peace. Moreover, Spain and Turkey, at either end of the Mediterranean, would be likely to take a

rolls after Montgomery's forces. (Right) A German killed in the retreat.

more pro-Allied posture as a result of the landings and a victory. Finally, dominating the Mediterranean itself would cut thousands of miles and months of time from Allied convoys' travel to Russia, the Middle and Far East.

If French military and civil authorities in North Africa cooperated, Allied troops could go swiftly through Morocco and Algeria, their rear and communications secure, and take the vital objective: Tunisia. Here, they could cut off Rommel's retreat or evacuation and finally crush him between their forces and Montgomery's Eighth Army.

If French forces did not resist, American and British troops would not be put in the awkward position of having to kill Frenchmen, and Allied casualties in the landings might be greatly minimized or perhaps even totally eliminated.

But French military and colonial administrations

Carrying a flag for identification, American troops go ashore in French

were anti-British, anti-democratic, and pro-Axis, and the Vichyite businessmen and landowners had important connections with Germany and Italy. Though most ordinary Frenchmen were pro-Allied, they were not in positions of power. There was still much bad blood between the French armed forces and the British. The French Navy remembered how the Royal Navy had smashed their fleet at Oran in 1940 after the fall of France. The French Army was bitter about the British military's invasion of Syria and their own defeat there. Nor had the British forgotten that these same Vichy French had turned their Syrian air bases over to the Nazis and then fought against the British who had attempted to secure them, that these same Vichy French had also fought them in Madagascar, turned Indochina over to the Japanese, and refused—at Oran, Alexandria, and Toulon—to bring their Navy over to the British side.

The Americans, however, had no such experience or

Morocco. At some points, the Vichy French troops put up a stiff resistance.

bad blood. To assure themselves of a friendlier reception from the French, it was decided therefore to give "Torch" an "American look." One of the ways of doing so was to make the expedition commander an American, in this case Lieutenant General Dwight D. Eisenhower. But the American complexion of "Torch" deprived it of British political experience in dealing with the wily Vichyites, and put the U. S. in the morally embarrassing position of an unprovoked assault on a "neutral" country.

Matters were further complicated by American and Vichyite attitudes toward General Charles de Gaulle and the Free French. The Vichy French looked on the Free French as traitors to France because the Gaullists had fought on against the Nazis instead of accepting the shameful surrender. The Free French looked on the Vichyites as traitors to France and Nazi collaborators. North African leaders—in the main Vichy appointees—were therefore hostile to de Gaulle and the Free French. The American attitude is more difficult to explain. Presumably the Americans were unwilling to enlist de Gaulle's aid because his own 1941 expedition against Vichyite Dakar had failed, possibly because news of it had "leaked" in advance from his London headquarters. Also, the U. S. believed that Vichyite hostility to the Free French would increase resistance to any invasion of North Africa which included the Gaullists, and would therefore mean more Allied casualties. In addition, both Americans and British found the haughty de Gaulle a difficult man to deal with. As a result the fateful decision was taken to exclude the Free French from the invasion and to attempt to enlist the aid of the Vichyite ruling group in North Africa. The Americans brought General Henri Honoré Giraud, a right-wing and anti-democratic military man, though with a record of bravery in fighting the Germans in both world wars, out of Vichy France in a submarine. They planned for him to be the leader around whom citizens and soldiers in North Africa would rally.

American diplomacy worked to enlist sympathy in North Africa. American political counselor Robert Murphy attempted to organize pro-Allied elements; Fleet Admiral William D. Leahy, former U. S. ambassador to Vichy, backed him up; and, three weeks before the actual landings, Lieutenant General Mark W. Clark undertook a long, dangerous submarine voyage to North Africa to batten down the last-minute arrangements which were to make certain that there would be no French resistance, or at most "token" opposition.

But the plans went awry. The Vichy French did resist and there was bloody fighting at Oran and Port Lyautey, while, at Casablanca, French fleet units and the unfinished battleship Jean Bart turned their guns on the American invasion force and had to be blasted by naval gunfire and dive-bombing. General Giraud at first insisted that he be put in command of the Allied expedition — in which there was not a single French soldier — and was then cold-shouldered by the French military and civil governors. By curious coincidence the notorious Axis collaborator and successor to Marshal Pétain, Admiral Darlan, was in Algiers, ostensibly visiting a son hospitalized with infantile paralysis. To tangle the skein still further, General Eisenhower was persuaded to deal with Darlan as the only man who could guarantee a swift cease-fire, maintain order behind the lines while the Allies lunged for Tunisia, and bring Tunisia and the French Fleet at Toulon over the Allies.

Darlan proved a slippery cohort. Twisting and turning, alternately resisting and giving way to Allied requests and threats, Darlan finally cloaked himself in

Pétain's authority—though repudiated by the old Marshal in a radio broadcast—and called for an armistice.

By then, however, the Allied armies had fought the French to a standstill and the French armies, battered and short of ammunition, had requested a cease-fire before Darlan's order went out. Under Darlan's aegis, however, French West Africa and its strategic port of Dakar did come over to the Allies, but Gaullists and others pointed out that Vichyite Governor-General Pierre Boisson had little alternative. Boxed in by the Allies in the north and de Gaulle's French Equatorial Africa on the south, he knew he could get more "sympathetic" treatment from Darlan than from de Gaulle.

Three days after the first landings, the fighting was over, and helped by Gaullists taking Algiers, British

American tanks move toward the enemy over typical North African terrain

Lieutenant General Kenneth Anderson's First Army sprinted along the coastal road for Tunisia. Commandos and parachutists were dropped at Bone, near Tebessa and Souk-el-Arba to seize advanced bases and airfields in Eastern Algeria. By November 25, Anderson's patrols had overrun strategic crossroads at Medjez-el-Bab, 30 miles southwest of Tunis, and it looked like the Allied gamble to take Tunisia might pay off.

Here, once more, working with Darlan failed to achieve its purpose. Darlan was supposed to order the pro-Axis chiefs in Tunisia, Resident-General Admiral Juan Esteva and commander of the Bizerte naval base, Admiral Edmond Louis Derrien, to join the Allies. Darlan at first refused, then stalled, and when he finally acquiesced — after being threatened with arrest — the

The open plains made advancing troops easy targets for enemy artillery.

Germans were already pouring troops into Tunisia and Vichy had ordered its commanders not to resist them.

The Nazis reacted to "Torch" with speed and dispatch. They flooded men and matériel into Tunisia and occupied Vichy France. Here, again, dealing with Darlan did not pay. He refused to give a clear order for the French battle fleet to sail from Toulon to join the Allies. When, on November 27, the Nazis tried to seize it, the fleet was scuttled by its crews. Some 73 ships were sent to the bottom of Toulon harbor, among them 1 battleship, 2 battlecruisers, 7 cruisers, and 29 destroyers. Nor did French fleet units at Dakar, Alexandria, and Bizerte choose to join the Allies; in fact, those at Bizerte went over to the enemy.

Ironically, though the Vichy French stubbornly fought the Allied landings, they did not resist Hitler's invasion of unoccupied France or of Vichyite Tunisia. As a result, the Germans were able to seize the only two all-weather airfields, outside Tunis and Bizerte. This automatically gave them air supremacy in Tunisia because the rainy season had come, washing out roads, making airfields seas of mud, and depriving the Allies of the use of those forward airstrips they had seized. The Luftwaffe slashed at Allied communication and supply lines, and the British First Army's advance was stopped on November 28 at Djedeida, only 12 miles from Tunis.

The First Army now had to pull back, but it held on to the vital Medjez-el-Bab, in spite of the German counterattack, though it was driven back 20 miles.

A wave of revulsion and a torrent of criticism swept the democratic countries at dealing with Darlan. On November 17, President Roosevelt was forced to make a public statement: "The present temporary arrangement in North and West Africa is only a temporary expedient, justified solely by the stress of battle." But this neither satisfied the critics nor encouraged co-operation from Darlan. Though the expedient had produced few significant results, Darlan was allowed to maintain most of the Vichy ruling caste in power, jail Gaullists and democrats, and retain in force Vichyite anti-labor and anti-Semitic laws.

Then, on the day before Christmas, a mysterious twenty-year-old Frenchman, Fernand Bonnier de la Chappelle, walked into Darlan's office, shot him twice, and within the hour, the admiral was dead. Twenty-four hours later, and without informing the Anglo-American Allies, a Vichyite court-martial had sentenced the youth to death and had him executed before a firing squad. Given another opportunity to remove the stigma of working with Vichyite Axis-collaborators, the Americans instead elevated General Giraud to Darlan's place. In all this, the British, who backed de Gaulle, went reluctantly but loyally along with their powerful ally.

Casablanca Conference

In January 1943, Roosevelt and Churchill met at Casablanca to lay plans for the next attacks on the Axis. Though invited, the Soviets did not attend, pleading the pressure of their winter counteroffensive, and once more lack of political and military coordination between the Anglo-Americans and the Russians was all too apparent. Plans were discussed and made for a cross-Channel invasion of Europe in 1944, for knocking Italy out of the war, for intensifying the bombing of Germany and the anti-U-boat campaign, and the Allied leaders somewhat belatedly tried to mend fences by bringing de Gaulle and Giraud together. But Giraud would not agree to eliminate Axis collaborators or rescind repressive Vichyite legislation.

At the Casablanca Conference: (from left to right) General
Henri Giraud, Roosevelt, General de Gaulle and Churchill.

The most important result of the Casablanca Conference was the Allied declaration that they would
accept only "unconditional surrender" from the Axis.
This was severely criticized as giving the Axis no choice
but to continue resistance, and Roosevelt himself in-
dicated that the phrase had only come to him acciden-
tally at the press conference. Nonetheless, both leaders
took the opportunity during 1943 to indicate that what
they meant need not be disastrous to those who surrendered. On June 30, 1943, Churchill said:

We, the United Nations, demand from the Nazi,
Fascist, and Japanese tyrannies unconditional surrender. By this we mean that their will power to resist

must be completely broken, and that they must yield themselves absolutely to our justice and mercy.... It does not mean, and it never can mean, that we are to stain our victorious arms by inhumanity or by mere lust of vengeance, or that we do not plan a world in which all branches of the human family may look forward to what the American Declaration of Independence finely calls "life, liberty, and the pursuit of happiness."

On December 24, 1943, President Roosevelt added: The United Nations have no intention to enslave the German people. We wish them to have a normal chance to develop in peace, as useful and respectable members of the European family. But we most certainly emphasize the word "respectable," for we intend to rid them once and for all of Nazism and Prussian militarism and the fantastic and disastrous notion that they constitute the "Master Race."

But Allied statements insisting on "unconditional surrender," whether calculated or accidental, whether modified in speeches or in fact, were to haunt all political and military negotiations with the Axis powers right up to the end of the war.

Victory in the Desert

By the end of January 1943, Rommel's Afrika Korps had pulled back to the Mareth line, the 20-mile-long Tunisian border fortifications the French had originally built against the Italians. Here, Rommel joined his 75,000 men to those of General Jurgen von Arnim, whose forces Hitler had built up to a strength of 100,000 since the "Torch" landings. Together, they were penned in an almost rectangular bridgehead about the size of the state of Pennsylvania: the southern

side faced the Eighth Army; the western faced the British First Army, the French 19th Corps, and the U. S. Army's II Corps; the other two sides of the rectangle faced the sea.

No sooner had Rommel arrived than he seized the initiative. At the end of January he lunged against the French at Faid Pass and then on February 14 he threw his new "Tiger" tanks against the still green Americans, inflicted heavy losses on them, and broke through their lines at Kasserine Pass. After being thrown back almost 55 miles, the British and Americans stopped his armor and beat him back the same distance. On March 6, Rommel turned on the Eighth Army and launched his

(Above) Montgomery meets Eisenhower to plan the spring offensive in Tunisia. The British attack was to come from the south, the American from the west. (Below) American infantrymen digging in for protection.

The final stages in Tunisia. (Below) British gunners score a direct hit on a Nazi Mark-II tank. (Above) Gurkhas on the assault with a Gurkha knife called the kurkri. (Left) Australians hit the dirt as a captured Nazi tank explodes.

Panzers at Medenine, Montgomery's main supply depot. Here, British anti-tank gunners stopped his tanks cold and left more than 50 of them hulks on the battlefield without losing a single one of their own.

Allied supplies had now been built up, and Allied communications strengthened. The African armies were now joined in a single command with Eisenhower at the head, and with British commanders — Alexander, Admiral Cunningham, and Air Marshal Tedder — in

Eighth Army men on the attack in Tunisia. The smoke blowing across th charge of ground, sea, and air operations respectively. At the same time, Allied planes, submarines, and naval units slammed Axis supply lines. On March 20, Montgomery went over to the offensive. One prong of his attack was a frontal assault on the Mareth line; the second was a flanking maneuver around Rommel's right wing. After a week of savage fighting, Rommel was forced to pull his troops back to avoid being cut off, and was shortly thereafter recalled to Germany. On

center of the picture is from a shellburst which the veterans scarcely notice.

April 7, the Allied armies joined hands and together battered the Axis salient. They now had overwhelming superiority in tanks, planes, and guns and in swift strokes they smashed the sides of the narrowing box into which the Axis troops were penned. The Eighth Army drove through two violently defended defense positions to reach Tunis on May 7; two days later the Americans had blasted their way into Bizerte. So rapidly did this happen, though with much precious Allied blood spilled, that both sides were surprised, as Alan Moorehead noted in entering Tunis:

Quite suddenly the Avenue de Bardo sprang to life. Crowds of French people rushed into the street and they were beside themselves in hysterical delight. Some rushed directly at us, flinging themselves on the running-boards. A girl threw her arms around my driver's neck. An old man took a packet of cigarettes from his pocket and flung them up at us. Someone else brandished a bottle of wine. All the women had flowers that they had hastily plucked up from their gardens. A clump of roses hit me full on the mouth and there were flowers all over the bonnet of the car. Everyone was screaming and shouting and getting in the way of the vehicles, not caring whether they were run over or not. . . . There were Germans walking about all over the place. They stood gaping on the pavements, standing in groups, just staring, their rifles slung over their shoulders. A Bren-gun carrier shot past us and it was full of Germans whom the Tommies had picked up, and in their excitement the crowd imagined that these Germans in the British vehicle were British and so they threw flowers at them. The Germans caught the flowers, and they sat there stiffly in the Bren-gun carrier, each man with a little posy clutched in his hand.

The double doors of a big red building on the right-hand side of the street burst open and at first I could not understand—the men who ran out, scores, hundreds of them, were British, in flat steel helmets and British battle-dress. Then it came to me—they were prisoners whom we had rescued. They stood in an undecided group for a moment on the sidewalk in the rain, filling their eyes with the sight of us. Then they cheered. Some of them had no heart to speak and simply looked. One man, bearded up to his eyes, cried quietly. The others yelled hoarsely. Suddenly the whole mass of men were swept with a torrent of emotional relief and wild joy. They yelled and yelled. . . .

Meanwhile another patrol of armored cars had taken the right fork, the Rue de Londres, down to the centre of the town. They took the city entirely unawares. Hundreds of Germans were walking in the streets, some with their girl friends. Hundreds more were sitting drinking apéritifs in a big pavement café. No one had warned them the British were near. The attack had gone so quickly that here in the town there had been no indication that the Axis line was broken. Now, suddenly, like a vision from the sky, appeared these three British armored cars. The Germans rose from their seats and stared. The Tommies stared back. There was not much they could do. Three armored cars could not handle all these prisoners. In the hair-dressing salon next door more Germans struggled out of the chairs and, with white sheets round their necks and lather on their faces, stood gaping.

The three armored cars turned back for reinforcements.

In this mad way Tunis fell that night. . . .

A brilliant tank maneuver cutting off all further possibility of resistance on Cap Bon, and an Allied aerial and naval blockade preventing evacuation by sea, forced the Axis to surrender. On May 12, German General Arnim and Italian Field Marshal Messe capitulated with all their troops. The war in Africa was finally over.

From its inception the African campaign had cost the Axis almost 1,000,000 men, killed and captured, 8000 planes, 6200 guns, 2500 tanks, 70,000 trucks, and almost 2,500,000 tons of shipping. In the Tunisian campaign alone, the Allies had killed, wounded, or captured more than 300,000 Axis soldiers, but there had also been 50,000 Allied casualties.

Soviet Counteroffensive

At Stalingrad, the Red Army crushed the last Nazi chance for victory in Russia. The major objectives of Hitler's 1942 campaign—the Caucasus, Stalingrad and Leningrad—remained in Russian hands and the cream of the Wehrmacht, the 20 divisions of Paulus's 6th Army, had been wiped out and could never be replaced.

The Red Army had taken a terrible toll in German men, machines, and matériel in the titanic struggle on the Eastern front. The Nazis had suffered 1,250,000 casualties in 1942, and though they had inflicted far greater losses on the Russians—the Soviets admitted 4,500,000 killed, wounded, and captured in the first year of their war—the Russians could replace their losses. As Russia grew stronger, helped by new and transplanted production beyond the Urals and by Anglo-American aid, the Germans grew weaker. Particularly in manpower the Russians could make good their losses, and here the Nazis, even with the use of slave labor and an increasingly rigid draft of younger and older Germans, could not fill the gaps.

No sooner had the Russians forced Paulus's surrender in the opening days of February 1943 when the Red Army hurled the remainder of the Wehrmacht back on its heels. In furious fighting it took Kursk and Byelgorod, and by mid-February had driven the Nazis from

These inadequate uniforms cost many German lives.

Russians using tommy guns to clean out pockets of Nazi resistance.

Kharkov and in early March forced Mannstein to evacuate Rzhev and Vyazma on the central front. Russian supply lines were now extended because they had pushed forward over 430 miles from Stalingrad in three months, and fresh German forces under the skillful Mannstein checked their advance and threw them back. On March 14 the Nazis recaptured Kharkov.

During the spring thaws, there was a lull in the fighting until July 5, when Hitler launched his summer offensive. Compared to the vast offensives in his two previous campaigns on the Eastern front, this was a much smaller-scale operation. Some 30 divisions comprising 500,000 men were thrown at a Russian salient which extended 60 miles west of Kursk into the German lines. Kluge and Mannstein threw their Panzers at the north and south flanks of this Kursk bulge respectively, hoping to pinch it off and annihilate the almost 1,000,000 Russian troops there. But the Red Army was prepared and its artillery smashed almost half the German tanks in what Russian General Ivan Koniev called the "swan song of the German Panzers." With its armored spearheads blunted, the Nazi thrust ground to a halt, having made only minor inroads on the salient. It was a devastating defeat. Not only had the Nazi reserves of men and armor been squandered, not only had their columns suffered 70,000 casualties and the loss of 1000 planes, but they were now off balance and open for the Red Army counterattack.

The Russians launched a general offensive on the whole central and southern front. Red Army groups under the new generation of Soviet generals—Sokolovsky, Popov, Vatutin, Rokossovsky, Koniev, Malinovsky, and Tolbukhin—now drove westward against stubborn Nazi resistance and pushed the Germans out of the key towns they had taken and held for more than a year and a half. During August and September 1943, Orel, Byelgorod, Taganrog, Stalino, Mariupol, Bryansk, and Poltava were recaptured. The Germans fell back, scorching the earth in their wake, to a line of fortifications they had built on the great bend of the Dnieper from Gomel down to the Sea of Azov. By the end of September, the Russians had captured the strategic rail and communications center of Smolensk, keystone of German defenses on the central front, and farther south had pushed to the Dnieper River on a broad 80-mile front from Kremenchug to Dniepropetrovsk. Still farther south, the Red Army had pushed Kleist's 14 divisions out of the last German bridgehead in the Kuban across the Kerch Straits into the Crimea.

In October, the Russians plunged across the Dnieper in three places. The advance in the north outflanked and captured Kiev on November 6, then Gomel, and struck for Zhitomir, which they recaptured on the twelfth. In the center, Red Army forces seized Dniepropetrovsk on October 5, and then lunged for Krivoi Rog. In the south, after savage fighting, the Russians recaptured Melitopol and on November 1, seized the Perekop Isthmus, blocking the 17th German Army in the Crimea from escape by land. German General Mellenthin described the fury of the Soviet advance:

The artillery bombardment was really quite impressive. No movement was possible, for 290 guns of all calibers were pounding a thousand yards of front, and during these two hours the Russians expended their normal ammunition allowance for one-and-a-half days. The bombardment reached as far back as divisional battle headquarters, and the two divisions holding the corps front were shelled with such intensity that it was impossible to gauge the Schwerpunkt. Some Russian guns fired over open sights from uncovered gun em-

141

The Russians (above) proved far better winter fighters than the Germans.

placements. After the two hours' bombardment our trench system looked like a freshly ploughed field, and in spite of being carefully dug in, many of our heavy weapons and anti-tank guns had been knocked out.

Suddenly Russian infantry in solid serried ranks attacked behind a barrage on a narrow front, with tanks in support, and one wave following the other. Numerous low-flying planes attacked those strong-points which were still firing. A Russian infantry attack is an

awe-inspiring spectacle; the long grey waves come pounding on, uttering fierce cries, and the defending troops require nerves of steel. . . .

One fateful evening he [General Dietrich von Choltitz] talked to me about the way things were going, and expressed anxiety at the terrific pressure on our front. Then he had a vision. He saw how the Soviet masses would close in on us like giant ocean waves. All the dams built to stem their onrush would be shattered

143

(Above) A Nazi rearguard surrendering to Red Army troops. (Below) A parade of German prisoners in Leningrad after the lifting of the seige.

and the Russians would go on and on and eventually submerge Germany. He wanted to go and see Hitler himself and tell him the facts. . . .

I did my best to convince the General by quoting sober figures, to show that even the flood of Russian manpower was bound to run dry. I pointed to the incredibly high losses the Russians had suffered at the hands of his corps, which had fought with unrivalled bravery and courage, and I told him that one day even the Russian attacks would peter out. My arguments made little impression and he remained unmoved in his decision. He did not believe that our front would hold on the following day. He wanted to spare his troops this terrible ordeal; they were growing weaker and weaker and there was no hope of getting replacements or reinforcements. The next morning he drove away from Corps Headquarters, still determined to put his views before Hitler.

Through winter snow and cold the Red Army onslaught continued unabated, giving the Germans no rest. At the beginning of 1944, a renewed offensive in the north finally lifted the siege of Leningrad and threw the Nazis back to Lake Peipus and the Estonian border. In February, the key positions in the Dnieper bend, Nikopol and Krivoi Rog, fell to advancing Russian columns. In March, with Marshals Zhukov and Vassilevski now in over-all command in the south, the Russians launched a vigorous spring offensive there which by the end of the month had thrown the Germans back into eastern Poland and early in April across the Romanian border too. On April 10, the Germans were forced to evacuate Odessa on the Black Sea and on April 8, the Russians attacked the Germans in the Crimea. In a little more than a month they had beaten down the garrison's last resistance.

The Long Roads to Victory

"Operation Husky"

Two months after the Axis surrender in Africa, on July 10, 1943, the Allies struck across the Mediterranean against Sicily. The same Allied team that had successfully beaten the Axis in Tunisia was in command—Eisenhower, Alexander, Tedder, and Cunningham—but there were serious differences on the Mediterranean operation. The Americans wanted to limit objectives so that the main Allied strength would be husbanded for the cross-Channel invasion—now code-named "Overlord"—tentatively scheduled for spring 1944. The British, on the other hand, with memories of the Somme and Passchendaele, and Dunkirk, seemed more disposed to continued attack on the "soft-underbelly" of Europe, up through Italy and perhaps the Balkans. A difference never fully resolved, it was to cost many Allied lives.

Preliminary air and naval bombardment had already subdued the islands between Sicily and North Africa—Pantelleria, Lampedusa, and Linosa—and the night before the seaborne landings, parachute and glider troops were dropped to seize airfields, and attack the troops defending beachheads from the rear. In spite of inexperience, which caused many gliders to be dropped in the sea and their troops drowned, the operation was a help and the parachutists and airborne troops did yeoman work before the landings.

"Husky" was the first large-scale amphibious operation against Europe and more than 3200 ships took part in ferrying 160,000 Allied troops across the Sicilian Straits. The American Seventh Army under Lieutenant General George S. Patton, Jr., landed on the northwest beaches between Licata and Scoglitti, the center of their beachhead at Gela. The British Eighth

Paratroops on their way to Sicily. Some were tragically killed when naval vessels shot down their transports.

Army, including a Canadian corps, landed on both sides of the southern tip of the island, on the U. S. right flank, between Pozzalo and Syracuse. Facing them were ten Italian and three and a half German divisions, some 400,000 troops, commanded by Field Marshal Albert Kesselring.

Except for one savage Nazi counterattack at the Gela beachhead, which the Americans beat back with the help of Royal Navy shelling, the landings went

swiftly and smoothly. Most of the Italians, who had
had their fill of both war and fascism, had no heart for
fighting and melted away. But three crack Nazi divisions—the Hermann Göring, the 15th Panzer Grenadier,
and the 29th Motorized—reinforced by tough parachutists were 90,000 strong. Patton drove north and
west and within three weeks overran all the western
half of Sicily. Montgomery's troops faced less resistance on the beachheads, quickly secured the necessary
port of Syracuse, but had rougher going thereafter.

The major Allied objective was to capture Messina,
the port directly across the narrow straits from the

Landing craft getting men and gear ashore at Sicily. Naval gunfire brilliantly broke up an attempted German counterattack by the battle-seasoned Hermann Göring Panzer division. (Below) Getting a jeep through sand.

Italian mainland, the only funnel of supplies and re-inforcements for the Germans and their only means of escape. Four roads led to Messina, two coastal routes from Palermo along the north shore of the island and from Syracuse along the east coast, and two inland routes, one through Troino, the other through Adrano, both of which joined at Randazzo. The British Eighth Army, driving up the shorter east-coast road, was a greater threat to Messina and the Germans concentrated their main strength against it. Moreover, the terrain there was favorable for defense. Heavily entrenched on 11,000-foot Mount Etna, the Nazis overlooked the Catanian plain and from their high ground held Montgomery's troops up for three weeks. Reinforced by mountain-fighting troops from Tunisia, Montgomery then sent his left flank around the western slopes of Mount Etna and drove up the inland road through Adrano toward Messina, while his right flank pushed up the coastal road on the east side of the mountain.

Though greatly outnumbered the Germans fought a fierce and skillful rear-guard action, contesting every inch of ground, and intent on getting as many of their troops out of Sicily as possible. So determined and tenacious was their resistance, that Patton's Seventh Army was several times forced to outflank rear-guards by making amphibious landings in their rear. On one of these, made on August 9 at Brolo, Jack Belden describes how the back of German resistance was broken.

We scaled the steep sides of our ducks [amphibious landing craft] and sitting on them much like a fireman on a hook and ladder we waited while our ship drew closer to shore. The air was suffocating. A man retched. A voice said, "That reminds me of the time I used to drink varnish remover," but no one laughed.

(Above) British troops against whom the Germans concentrated the greater part of their strength. (Below) Typical pillboxes from which the troops had to root machine guns.

In the impenetrable gloom we could see nothing, only a tiny light that hung in the blackness above us. At that moment there was the muffled sound of a moving mechanism. The great ramp door opened slightly. A gray patch of light crept into the ship. We sat on the decks and watched the widening streak and wondered what was behind that slowly falling door. . . . Now we looked into the twinkling eyes of the sky. Now we saw the craggy peak of Mount Brolo. Now the lower

Crowds in the streets of Palermo, Sicily, celebrate the arrival of the firs

hips of the hills. Now the moist mouth of the sea.

Our duck slid into the water and swam effortlessly toward shore. The underwater exhaust made almost no sound. Ahead a destroyer close in shore loomed menacing, her guns silent but ready. We threw her a grateful glance and passed on.

From the beach two yellow lights like fallen stars shone to seaward. Our engineers had marked well the goal and we headed confidently toward it. Then some-

American troops. The city surrendered on July 23, without firing a shot.

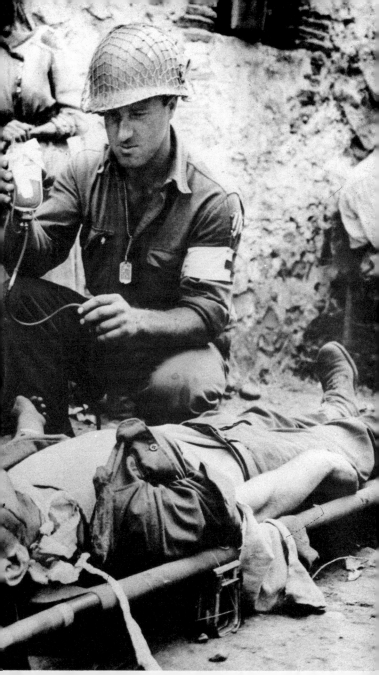

There were 10 Italian divisions on Sicily, but most of them had lost heart for

where inland a shower of sparks sprayed the darkness with orange and red balls. Ours or the enemy's explosion? It didn't matter. Surprise was gone.

We cut out the underwater exhaust. Motors roared wide open. With spray flying our ducks thrashed for the beach. With a sudden churning they rose from the sea and shaking themselves free from spray reared on to dry land. It was exactly 3:15. . . .

"Get out! Get out!" shouts Major Fargo, battalion

...hting. (Above) General Keyes accepts the surrender of an Italian general.

executive officer.

We vault to the ground. Blindly, feet plowing through sand, we follow Fargo. Barbed wire clutched at us. Snip, snip go the wire cutters and we are free and move on.

Duck low to get off the skyline. Pass over a railway embankment. Slide down into someone's garden. Walk into a narrow irrigation ditch. Teeter like a tight-rope walker. Seek to hold your balance. I suppress a desire to laugh. Perhaps I am getting battle-wacky.

Now we reach a lemon grove. Figures flit through the blackness. Voices whisper, "Where's G Company? Where's F Company? Where's the road? Where's the hill?"

"Keep moving!" We turn to the right, halt. . . .

Turning sharply to the left where we heard the rustling sound of moving figures we came up against a line of barbed wire. As we paused a rifle shot snapped overhead. Firing instantly broke out from all sides. Ours or the enemy's—what was the difference?—either's bullets could kill us. We threw ourselves to the ground. A sergeant named Daily who had joined us snipped at the barbed wire and we crawled through and sheltered behind a stone wall. I no longer felt like laughing. . . .

Put, put put! A mobile globule of sound was approaching down the road. A motorcycle. Instantly rifle fire whistled up from the roadside. Tires shrieked on macadam. A motor raced violently, then died.

Now the sound of several motors roared toward us. We waited in ambush beneath the wall, taut and silent. Like a crackling fire, rifles and machine guns split the air. Lined in the shooting light of tracer bullets we saw wheel spokes and the red flashes of bullets shooting through them.

A louder explosion shook the wall where we huddled. Lieutenant Thomas Rodgers was firing his anti-tank weapon. A flash of flame tore the darkness and spotlighted a careening truck and the white frightened face of the driver.

Then the dark night doused the flame again and in the blackness a crash sounded, glass broke and a man shrieked.

The night was upside down with shouts, bullets and

moving figures. We could not know what was happening. A private clapped his hand on somebody's shoulder and said: "What unit you from, buddy?" A voice answered, "Mein Gott!" A pistol shot rang out; some one howled and then gurgled.

The Germans, under cover of darkness and a heavy curtain of anti-aircraft fire, managed to extricate more than 60,000 of their more than 90,000 troops, and most of their equipment, across the Messina Strait to the Italian mainland. On August 17, after 39 days of fierce fighting, Patton's columns entered Messina, then Montgomery's, and Sicily had been conquered. Allied losses had been 31,000 killed, wounded, and missing, for 37,000 German and 130,000 Italian casualties.

It had been a brief, if bitter, campaign which had accomplished its objectives. The Mediterranean was now cleared for Allied traffic through the Sicilian narrows; a springboard for invasion of Italy was secured and Italy had been knocked out of the war.

Italy Surrenders

Two weeks after the landings in Sicily and in the midst of the battle for the island, Mussolini was overthrown. On July 24, at the first Fascist Grand Council meeting convened in almost 20 years, the Duce was forced to resign by a 19–7 vote. A new government under Marshal Pietro Badoglio arrested Mussolini and immediately sent out feelers to the Allies for an armistice. From late July to early September, intricate negotiations took place between Badoglio's emissaries and the Allies as the Italians stalled, trying to negotiate better terms than "unconditional surrender." Knowing that the Allies were going to land at Salerno on September 9, Eisenhower forced Badoglio's hand by a second bombing of the railroad marshaling yards in Rome, and on September 3, a secret armistice was finally signed at Syracuse in Sicily.

But the long-drawn-out negotiations had given the Nazis all the time they needed to prepare and they now reacted promptly and decisively. Hitler's armies seized the government, strategic ports, airfields and other installations, and secured Rome and the industrial Po Valley in the north. The Wehrmacht swiftly disarmed the 30 Italian divisions in Italy and disarmed and replaced the 25 Italian divisions on garrison duty in the Balkans, thus putting even further strain on their already overextended armies. A daring, glider-borne landing in Abruzzi by Nazi commando forces under Otto Skorzeny rescued Mussolini on September 12, and Hitler was then able to use the great Number One to set up a rump Fascist regime in Nazi-occupied Italy.

Although the prolonged wrangling about armistice terms probably frustrated a quick and relatively bloodless Allied take-over of most of the Italian peninsula, the surrender itself did have other important results. All Italian armed forces did put down their arms. The Italian air force, merchant marine and, most important, the Italian Navy were turned over to the Allies. On the night of September 8, the Italian battle fleet sailed from its bases at Genoa, Spezia, and Taranto for Malta. Although Luftwaffe bombers sank one battleship and damaged a second; the Allies got the bulk of the fleet, including 5 battleships, 7 cruisers, and 6 destroyers. Sardinia and Corsica were also quickly overrun, but nowhere was there large-scale and effective resistance to the Germans by Italian armed forces or by the Italian populace. The Germans, consequently, were able to take over the country, commandeer what they needed, and continue to fight against the Allies on Italian soil.

Carrying pictures of the King, crowds celebrate the end of fascism.

The Allies supported the Badoglio government and King Victor Emmanuel, presumably to avoid Fascist revival, chaos, and Communism. Churchill wrote to Roosevelt that "There is nothing between the King, and the patriots who have rallied round him, who have complete control, and rampant Bolshevism." But neither Badoglio nor the King had any credit with liberal, democratic, and anti-Fascist forces in Italy, either leaders like Count Carlo Sforza and Benedetto Croce, or with the nameless author of this leaflet which greeted the Allied liberators:

Brothers,

After thirtynine months of war, pains and grieves; after twenty years of tiranny and inhumanity, after have the innocent victims of the most perverce gang at the Government; today, September 8, 1943, we can cry at full voice our joys our enthusiasm for your coming.

We can't express with words our pleasure, but only we kneel ourself to the ground to thank Good, who have permit us to see this day.

With you we have divided the sorrow of the war, with you we wish to divide the day of the big victory.

We wish to march with you, until the last days against the enemy N.1.

We will be worth of your expectation, we will be your allied of twentyfive years ago

Hurra the allied

Hurra the free Italy

> **The committee of antifascist
> exfighters of the big war**

But if Churchill saw only the menace of Bolshevism, many saw Allied policy repeating its North African precedent of supporting rightist, pro-Fascist and "legitimist" governments, and were deeply perturbed by it.

In any event, the Allies now accepted the Italians as co-belligerents, and on October 13, the Badoglio government declared war on Nazi Germany.

The Invasion of Italy

The protracted haggling with Badoglio over armistice terms forced a change in Allied strategy for invading Italy. Initially, Allied plans called for three simultaneous strokes: an airborne drop on Rome to seize its airfields; a seaborne landing near Naples to take that strategic port; and an invasion across the Messina Straits into Calabria, the toe of the Italian boot. The Allied armies scarcely paused after conquering Sicily. After 16 days of Allied planes pounding airfields, railroads, and communications, on September 3, two Eighth Army divisions moved across the Messina Strait to seize a 10-mile bridgehead on the Italian toe between Catonia and Reggio Calabria.

On the ninth, in a daring maneuver, the Royal Navy ferried the British 1st Airborne Division right into the harbor of Taranto and took that important naval base without opposition, its installations virtually intact. By the twelfth the Eighth had two other fine Adriatic ports, Bari and Brindisi, and 10 airfields in its hands.

On the ninth, too, the half-American, half-British Fifth Army under command of General Mark W. Clark hit the beaches on the Gulf of Salerno south of Naples and in the German rear. The Nazis expected them and were already dug into the heights dominating the beaches, raked the landings with fire and pinned the Fifth to the beachhead. Field Marshal Albert Kesselring, commanding the Wehrmacht in Italy south of Rome, concentrated five Panzer divisions against Clark's men and on September 11 threw dive bombers,

Salerno was a bad beach with German ME 109 fighters flying over the hills to pepper the attackers with machine-gun fire (above). Enemy tanks almost broke through to the water's edge, but the anti-tank gunners (below) pushed them back, and accurate naval gunfire worked over their attack routes.

heavy artillery, and the new radio-controlled and glider bombs against the Allies to drive them into the sea. The Nazis did push to within three miles of the sea, but the Allied air force and the Royal Navy were thrown into the breach. Admiral Cunningham moved his battleships close inshore to support the Fifth with naval gunfire, and the air force flew almost 2000 air strikes in a single day to blunt the German drive. The British battleship Warspite and the American cruisers Philadelphia and Savannah were damaged by glider bombs, but the beachhead was saved.

In the meantime, the Eighth Army raced up through Calabria and Apulia against only slight rearguard opposition. On the sixteenth its advanced spearheads joined the right wing of the Fifth, and together they threw Kesselring's Panzers back. On September 29, the Eighth took Foggia, and on October 1, the Fifth pushed into the ruins of Naples. The two strategic objectives of the first part of the campaign had been taken—the major port, though badly damaged by German demolitions, and the major airfields—and more than 200 miles up the Italian peninsula had been taken in three weeks.

Two factors now came into play: Italian geography and Allied differences on the Mediterranean campaign. The Apennines are the mountainous backbone of the Italian peninsula and any invader from the south must fight his way 600 miles northward along its slopes and over its peaks. Everywhere along the route, rivers, defiles, gorges, and ravines offer obstructions which, when skillfully fortified and defended, offer formidable opposition to any Allied advance. These natural obstacles built into Nazi defense lines each had to be stormed frontally in a war of attrition that was slow and painfully costly in human life.

Rangers climbing the hills which taxed the Allies during the campaign.

To move up the Italian peninsula swiftly, these positions had to be outflanked by amphibious landings, but neither troops nor landing craft for such operations were available. Committed as they were to the invasion of France in spring 1944, the Americans insisted that troops and landing craft be sent to England for that operation. They agreed to support British stress on a continued push up through Italy only if the forces there could make do with what they had.

To add to these difficulties, autumn rains swelled the rivers to torrents and left the roads muddy bogs. Then winter cold, snow, and ice made the troops even more miserable. It was a bitter war in Italy and Ernie Pyle tried to tell Americans back home what it was like for the fighting men:

The war in Italy was tough. The land and the weather were both against us. It rained and it rained. Vehicles bogged down and temporary bridges washed out. The country was shockingly beautiful, and just as shockingly hard to capture from the enemy. The hills rose to high ridges of almost solid rock. We couldn't go around them through the flat peaceful valleys, because the Germans were up there looking down on us, and they would have let us have it. So we had to go up and over. A mere platoon of Germans, well dug in on a high, rock-spined hill, could hold out for a long time against tremendous onslaughts. . . .

Our troops were living in almost inconceivable misery. The fertile black valleys were knee-deep in mud. Thousands of the men had not been dry for weeks. Other thousands lay at night in the high mountains with the temperature below freezing and the thin snow sifting over them. They dug into the stones and slept in little chasms and behind rocks and in half-caves. They lived like men of prehistoric times,

(Above) British infantry advances through wreckage typical of many Italian towns caught in the path of the war. (Below) Two men take cover from enemy fire as the truck at right and a second in the left rear are hit.

(Above) French troops which made up part of the international — American, Polish, Greek, British, New Zealand and Indian — Allied force in Italy. The men at left are goumiers from North Africa, those at the right belong to the regular French forces. (Below, left) A 240-mm howitzer — part of the assemblage of artillery brought up to beat down resistance in country not suitable for tanks. (Below, right) One of the mule trains which hauled ammunition up and wounded men down the rugged Italian mountains.

An Italian refugee child crying because her mother has just been injured.

and a club would have become them more than a machine gun. How they survived the dreadful winter at all was beyond us....

Our artillery prevailed—and how! We were prodigal with ammunition against those rocky crags, and well we might be, for a $50 shell could often save ten lives in country like that. Little by little, the fiendish rain of explosives upon the hillsides softened the Germans. They always were impressed by and afraid of our artillery, and we had concentrations of it there that were demoralizing.

And lastly, no matter how cold the mountains, or how wet the snow, or how sticky the mud, it was just as miserable for the German soldier as for the American.

Trench foot comes from a man's being wet and cold for long periods and from not taking off his shoes often enough. In the mountains the soldiers sometimes went for two weeks or longer without ever having their shoes off or being able to get their feet dry. The tissues gradually seem to go dead, and sores break out. It is almost the same as the circulation stopping and the flesh dying. In extreme cases gangrene occurs. We had cases where amputation was necessary. And in others soldiers couldn't walk again for six months or more....

The fighting on the mountaintop almost reached the caveman stage sometimes. Americans and Germans were frequently so close that they actually threw rocks at each other. Many more grenades were used than in any other phase of the Mediterranean war. And you have to be pretty close when you throw hand grenades.

Dead men have been coming down the mountain all evening, lashed onto the backs of the mules. They came lying belly-down across the wooden pack-saddles,

175

Part of the British-American force going ashore on the Anzio beachhead.

their heads hanging down on one side, their stiffened legs sticking out awkwardly from the other, bobbing up and down as the mules walked.

The Italian mule skinners were afraid to walk beside dead men, so Americans had to lead the mules down that night.

The next target was Rome, but south of it Kesselring had dug in behind powerful winter defenses on the Gustav line which ran along the Garigliano River, and its tributary the Rapido, to Monte Cassino, across the Apennines, and over to the Sangro River on the Adriatic coast. The key to the entire line was Monte Cassino

Planned to flank the Germans out of Cassino, it stalled into bitter fighting.

from whose 1100-foot heights the Germans commanded the approaches to the Liri Valley and to Rome. Atop the mountain was the ancient Monastery of St. Benedict which, though not fortified, was a perfect observation post from which the Germans could spot every Allied move in the valleys and fire on it.

Just before the end of the year, Eisenhower was transferred to England to become Supreme Allied Commander of "Overlord," and British General Henry Maitland Wilson replaced him in the Mediterranean. Air Marshal Tedder and Generals Patton, Bradley, and Montgomery were also assigned to "Overlord," and

therefore Lieutenant General Oliver Leese took charge
of the British Eighth Army and Lieutenant General Ira
C. Eaker assumed command of the Mediterranean Air
Forces. Lieutenant General Jacob Devers was brought
from England to take overall command of the American
forces, while Major General Mark Clark was in tactical
command of the U.S. Fifth Army. Admiral Andrew
Cunningham, who had served so brilliantly in the Mediterranean from the very beginning of the war, returned
to London to become First Lord of the Admiralty and
Admiral John Cunningham took over his job. The Germans also made command changes, moving Rommel
from command of forces north of Rome to France,
where he was to prepare for the anticipated Allied

**Wounded being brought back during the frustrating fighting
near Cassino. The Germans clung to the summit of the hill.**

landings, and the Italian front was turned over to Field Marshal Kesselring.

Before the bulk of his landing craft should also have to be sent to Britain for the priority "Overlord," General Harold Alexander, Allied ground comander, decided to assault the Gustav line frontally and simultaneously turn its right flank by an amphibious landing in its rear. On January 12, 1944, the Fifth Army hit the Gustav line frontally and 10 days later, at 2 A.M., a combined British-American assault force landed on the beaches at Anzio and Nettuno, 60 miles behind the Gustav line and only 36 miles south of Rome.

The landings were a complete tactical surprise, but though the road to Rome lay open—German General

A mortar outfit in action at Cassino. Shelling and bombing produced more rubble in which the Germans took cover.

Westphal testified that only two German battalions stood between the Allies at Anzio and Rome — the American commander, Major General John P. Lucas, delayed, cautiously consolidating his foothold on the beaches instead of audaciously thrusting for Rome, and also neglecting to seize the heights which commanded the beachhead. For almost a week Lucas did not try to break out of the bridgehead and by then it was too late. Kesselring, responding with characteristically swift efficiency, had two divisions on the high ground firing on the beaches within 48 hours. By February 1, he had concentrated 9 divisions against the 4 the Allies had pushed ashore, and was trying to drive their 70,000 troops into the sea.

British and American infantrymen, artillerymen, and tankmen fought desperately, aided by a withering Allied aerial bombardment and furious naval supporting fire — 2 Allied cruisers and 2 destroyers were lost off

Monte Cassino (below) in the early stages of the fighting before bombing had

Anzio—and finally stopped the Nazi counterattack. But though the tide had been stemmed, Kesselring had also succeeded in penning the Allies inside a small defense perimeter and so contained the threat to his rear and to Rome.

The Allies now had to break the impasse at Cassino where the pivotal position in the German defenses remained "Monastery Hill," or Hill 516, as it was more prosaically marked on artillery maps. In January and February 1944, two bitter battles were fought to break through the fanatical resistance of the Nazi 1st Parachute Division, but though the Benedictine Abbey on Monte Cassino was almost leveled by 500 Allied bombers the German lines held all during that long, bitter winter. Not until spring 1944 did the disastrous fighting before Cassino reach its climax. Preceded by a massive month-long air assault on Nazi supply and communication lines, the Fifth and Eighth Armies

turned it to rubble (below). The Nazis used the Abbey as an observation post.

(Above) A line of captured German prisoners files by the foxholes of U. S. infantrymen. (Below) Fifth Army troops join with men of the Anzio beachhead garrison. The way was now clear for an assault on defenses guarding Rome.

lunged against the Gustav line on May 11. By May 17, Imperial and Polish troops had cut off and taken Cassino, and on the 23rd breached the Gustav line defenses. Pushing north they were joined by the Anzio garrison which had broken out of its perimeter on May 17. Together their spearheads pierced the Hitler line, 12 miles behind the Gustav, and then, in furious fighting at Cisterna, Velletri, and Valmontone, burst through the last defenses before Rome. Allied columns now converged on Rome, which the Germans had declared an open city and left undamaged in their retreat, plunging through the Alban Hills to enter Rome on June 4, two days before the Allies were to strike across the Channel to invade Normandy.

Less than a year after landing in Sicily, Italy's capital and the first city of the Rome-Berlin-Tokyo Axis had fallen. It was poetic justice that it had been made possible by a truly international Army which included Americans, British, Canadians, French, New Zealanders, Indians, and Poles. And it was both a note of triumph and a warning of things to come when President Roosevelt declared: "one down and two to go."

The Long Roads to Tokyo

Not only had the Japanese misunderstood the temper of the American people when they bombed Pearl Harbor, they had also underestimated how rapidly America's productive capacity could replace the losses sustained there. Even with priority given to the European war, the U.S. was still able to fight effectively in the Pacific. At the beginning of 1943, with Guadalcanal and the southeastern tip of New Guinea secured, American strength really began to make itself felt.

Japan's defense perimeter, concentric rings of island

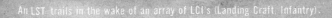
An LST trails in the wake of an array of LCI's (Landing Craft, Infantry).

bastions in the Pacific, now began to be pierced on all sides. Allied strategy called for four strikes through the outer defense rings. The first was an attack in the north Pacific to reconquer the Aleutians. The second was an advance in the Southwest Pacific by General MacArthur along the northern coast of the second largest island in the world, 1300-mile-long New Guinea. From there, the Philippines were the next stop. The third was Admiral Halsey's South Pacific forces to drive north through the Solomon Islands, and the last was Admiral Nimitz's task forces to smash through the Gilbert and Marshall Islands in the Central Pacific. The immediate targets were Japan's major bastions in the Central and Southwest Pacific: Rabaul on New Britain and Truk in the Caroline Islands. MacArthur and Halsey's troops would comprise a giant pincers coming up on either side of Rabaul, neutralizing it, and then choking it off altogether. Once that was completed, a second pincers would be developed: MacArthur would leapfrog to the Philippines; Halsey and Nimitz would converge on Japan's inner defense ring—the Marianas.

A brilliant amphibious variation of the age-old military tactic of envelopment was worked out. Allied forces would bypass Japanese strong points, landing on adjacent and relatively weakly defended areas. Here they would build an airfield and anchorage and, with control of sea and air, proceed to cut off the supply lines of the bypassed Japanese, gradually starving them out. To make such a series of "hit 'em where they ain't" amphibious "leapfrog" operations possible an armada of assault and landing craft, aircraft carriers, troop transports, supply ships, battleships, cruisers, and destroyers were necessary. Now, for the first time, the rapidly built American "two-ocean" Navy was able to provide them.

After Guadalcanal and Buna-Gona, Pacific operations paused until spring and summer of 1943. In May, American forces bypassed Kiska, the Japanese stronghold in the western Aleutians, and stormed ashore on Attu. In savage fighting, the Americans wiped out a garrison of 2350 men. With an American air base on Amchitka, 70 miles east of Kiska, organized in January, and Attu occupied in May, Kiska was effectively blockaded so the Japanese decided to evacuate it. In a clever and undiscovered maneuver in July, their Navy re-embarked the Kiska garrison and abandoned the island to the Americans, who occupied it in August. After only a year in Japanese hands, the Aleutians had

A Coast Guard gunner ready to fire as his landing craft noses in for the invasion of another Japanese-held Pacific island.

now been retaken, but biting cold and vile weather made them poor advanced bases for anything more than occasional bombing raids on the Japanese Kuriles.

In February, as part of the Guadalcanal operation, Admiral Halsey had begun his climb up the rungs of the Solomons "ladder" by seizing the Russell Islands, 60 miles northwest of Guadalcanal. At the end of June his forces landed on Rendova to bring the Japanese airfield at Munda, on New Georgia Island, under artillery fire. After heavy shelling and bombing, the Americans leaped to New Georgia to take Munda airfield itself. As in all the fighting in the steaming jungles of New Guinea and the Solomons, Americans and Australians found a tenacious, treacherous and courageous enemy who usually fought to the death. A night engagement on New Georgia is described by Australian newspaperman Osmar White in the Munda campaign.

The moon of New Georgia is very bright and in its light the forest was a stark, speckled black and white. The insect chorus diminished. The cry of the hunting birds was more abrupt and harsh. Then a new sound came out of the cold, white moonlight — the sound of Japanese voices, shrill and high-toned. . . .

Even though the first bursts of our guns must have pinpointed our perimeter positions clearly, the enemy was still uncertain of our strength and disposition. They sent in close reconnaissance.

One Japanese hid himself in a gully about 30 yards out and began squalling ludicrously: "Aid, aid, doc! Give aid to me. I am wounded!" He just screamed the words because he had been taught to scream them, parrot fashion. Their pitch was blood-chilling as the cry of an epileptic. A few nights before the troops might have fired on him, and the muzzle flashes would have betrayed their position. Not now.

Apart from the noise made by the squalling "tactician" in the deadfall, the stillness of the jungle now became deathly. The birds were quiet. Even the frog chorus seemed hushed. Inch by inch I lifted my head. One rustle and a grenade might have been tossed at me out of a bush, but I couldn't stand the blindness any more. I peered over the parapet.

In a little patch of moonlight about 15 yards away a Japanese soldier was standing upright, as still as a statue. I could see the shapeless folds of his uniform, the rifle he held, the glint of the bayonet, the peaked, soddy cap on his head. I saw him and perhaps twenty other men saw him—but no one fired. We knew he stood there deliberately inviting death, for a reason.

Somewhere behind him were two or three of his comrades with grenades ready. If anyone had fired they would have lobbed the grenades at the flash. Four or five Americans might have died in exchange for one Japanese life.

I would have liked the courage to keep watching the human bait while he waited for honorable death, but I lacked it. Inch by inch I put my head down.

There was a soft, metallic click. The man lying across my knees cocked his pistol. I twisted my mouth against his ear and breathed: "Don't shoot! Grenades!"

He whispered back: "Only if he jumps into the hole. They've been doing that lately." But he didn't jump in.

The posts on the jeep track opened up furiously for thirty seconds. This time the screams were genuine. Afterwards the man who had been screeching "Aid, aid!" withdrew to a greater distance and began imitating the cry of a stabbed man, calling after each shriek: "Christ, he's got me in the guts! I'm stabbed! Water, water!"

He kept this up for half an hour at 30- or 40-second

(Above) The dense jungle growth on many of the islands gave cover to both the invaders and Japanese snipers. (Left) These are not paratroopers, but para-bombs being dropped on a Japanese air field. They burst over their targets.

intervals. Then he crept in close again and began calling: "Buddy, are you there? Please, please answer me!"

The main body of the enemy, still a hundred yards away, broke out chattering anew. They had suffered sobering losses. They abandoned close attack and put snipers in the trees. Every few seconds there would be a sharp whack and a bullet would come singing out of the thickets. One or two Japanese, working alone, edged up and threw grenades blindly. Two bounded off the earth at the ends of our foxhole and exploded, but no one was even scratched.

By the first week in August, Munda was secured and by the end of the month organized resistance was over. Large-scale sea and air battles were fought for control of the central Solomons at the same time—two naval

American cruisers and destroyers going in toward a Japanese-held island.

engagements in Kula Gulf and one off Kolombangara–
in which naval losses were about equal on both sides,
but planes shot down favored the Americans 3 to 1.
On August 15, Halsey's troops leapfrogged to Vella
Lavella, bypassing heavily fortified Kolombangara and
its Vila air base, but the Japanese succeeded, after
losing 3 destroyers in the Battle of Vella Gulf, in skillfully evacuating almost 10,000 men from their Kolombangara garrison in early October. Simultaneously,
they withdrew from Santa Isabel and pulled most of
their troops out of Choiseul. On October 9, the Allies
took Barokoma airfield on Vella Lavella, 349 miles from
Rabaul, but not before a Japanese naval victory in the
Battle of Vella Lavella once more permitted them to
save their small garrison there by evacuation. All the
central Solomons were in Allied hands after a four-

month campaign in which the U.S. Navy had lost 6 warships, but had sunk 17 Japanese naval vessels — 2 light cruisers, 10 destroyers, and 5 submarines.

Halsey now knifed into the northern Solomons, by-passing the Shortland Islands, and flanking them by landing New Zealand troops to take the Treasury Islands on October 26. After a feint at Choiseul, the 3rd Marine Division was landed on the west coast of Bougainville on November 1. Almost 60,000 Japanese soldiers and sailors guarded Bougainville and its adjacent islands, but the Marines went ashore on the relatively lightly defended beaches along Empress Augusta Bay. Here was a good harbor and room for the two air strips the Allies built at Piva and Torokina. These not only neutralized the three Japanese airfields on 130-mile-long Bougainville but also provided an advanced air base against Rabaul, only 210 miles away. No attempt was made to do more than hold a protective perimeter around the airfields and naval anchorage; the remainder of the island was left to the Japanese. Two fierce naval battles—at Empress Augusta Bay on November 25 and at Cape St. George on November 25— were fought in which the Japanese suffered heavy losses, but they could neither halt the American landings nor make effective counterattacks.

On February 14, Halsey leapfrogged to Green Island, north of Bougainville, thus cutting off all the Japanese bases in northern Bougainville, and on Buin and Buka. On Green Island, Allied fighters were only 120 miles east of Rabaul and flanked the Japanese bastion's main supply line to Truk, 700 miles to the north. The right wing of the Allied pincers around Rabaul was now complete.

In the meantime, the left wing of the pincers was simultaneously moving up New Guinea's north coast. In a series of brilliant combined amphibious, parachute, and airborne assaults, MacArthur landed troops on both flanks of the Lae-Salamaua salient, cutting the Japanese garrisons there off from reinforcements and supplies. Two Australian divisions then closed in with American air and naval support, and after a series of hard-fought battles, drove into Lae on September 11, captured Salamaua five days later, and on October 2 seized Finschhafen. By mid-November the Huon Peninsula had been overrun.

Before moving farther along the New Guinea coast, MacArthur turned to secure his right flank, command the sea exit north from the Coral Sea and to close in further on Rabaul from the east. Facing New Guinea's Huon Peninsula across the 63-mile-wide Dampier and Vitiaz Straits is the 250-mile-long island of New

196

Paratroops landing in support of men already ashore on Noemfoor Island in the Pacific. (Below) Typical jungle fighting. The Japanese were excellent snipers skilled at concealment in branches of trees and in foxholes.

Britain at whose northeast tip is Rabaul. In December, MacArthur sent elements of the U.S. Sixth Army under General Walter Krueger to seize Arawe on the south coast of New Britain and also had the 1st Marine Division under General William Rupertus make an amphibious strike on the northwestern end of the island to seize the Cape Gloucester airfields which commanded the Dampier and Vitiaz Straits. Fighting in a sea of mud, torrential rains, and jungle as dense and dark as Guadalcanal's, the Marines took Cape Gloucester and then moved up the north coast in mid-March to Willaumez Peninsula where they captured the airstrip at Talasea. They were now only 160 air miles from Rabaul and the western end of New Britain was secure in Allied hands.

Two more amphibious assaults completed the ring of air and naval bases that were a noose around Rabaul's neck. In early March, Manus and Los Negros Islands in the Admiralties were taken, 250 miles northeast of New Guinea, and shortly thereafter Emirau, northwest of New Ireland. The Allies now had bases astride the communication and supply lines from Rabaul and Kavieng to Truk from east and west.

Allied air forces in the Solomons and New Guinea now combined to bomb Rabaul, its harbors, airfields, shipping, and airplanes. A continuing day-by-day air assault, aided by carrier strikes from Halsey's Task Force 38, gradually throttled Rabaul and Kavieng. By the end of spring 1944 they had been effectively neutralized.

MacArthur now turned back to New Guinea. In a series of long-distance amphibious leapfrogs, he moved up the island's coast. Three U.S. divisions shuttled 600 miles west to take Hollandia and Aitape at the end of April, bypassing strong Japanese garrisons at Wewak and Hansa Bay. On May 27, MacArthur lunged 330 miles still farther west to seize Biak Island off the New Guinea northwest coast, and at the end of July, made his last leap to the western end of New Guinea to seize Sansapor. MacArthur was now only 600 miles from the Philippines.

After two years of bitter fighting in dense jungles, enduring tropical heat and disease, and against a relentless opponent, the Allies had come the 1300-mile length of the island from Milne Bay to Sansapor and left some 135,000 Japanese troops stranded and isolated in their wake. The campaign was over.

Tarawa: Blood on the Coral

After Vice-Admiral Thomas C. Kinkaid took the Aleutians, and while MacArthur and Halsey battered their way up through New Guinea and the Solomons, Admiral Nimitz moved through the Central Pacific to neutralize the Japanese air and naval base of Truk in the Carolines. American amphibious assault experience had been on the beaches of jungle-covered South Pacific islands; experience in invading a Central Pacific atoll, a strip of coral islands, islets and reefs that fringed an enclosed lagoon, was quite another matter. To gain that experience, the United States was to pay heavily on the bloody beaches of Tarawa in the Gilbert Islands.

The Gilberts lie 1100 miles northeast of Guadalcanal and 2500 miles southwest of Hawaii. A British Crown Colony, they were seized by the Japanese a few days after Pearl Harbor. The Japanese then built a seaplane base on Makin Atoll and an air field on a tiny coral islet, Betio, in the southwest corner of Tarawa atoll. These two were now the main targets of Nimitz's V Amphibious Corps, commanded by Rear Admiral Richmond K. Turner. The ground troops, led by Marine Corps Major General Holland M. ("Howlin' Mad") Smith, were in two task forces: the green Army 27th Infantry Division commanded by Major General Ralph C. Smith, was assigned to invade Makin; the 2nd Marine Division, veterans of Guadalcanal and Tulagi, commanded by Major General Julian C. Smith, were to take Tarawa.

In the 15 months following Pearl Harbor the Japanese had turned the less than square mile of Betio into a maze of formidable fortifications. Reef, beaches, and the islet itself were an elaborate combination of obstacles, mines, barbed wire, and gun emplacements with overlapping fields of fire. The beaches were raked by everything from rifle, machine-gun, and mortar fire to coastal defense gun shellfire. So skillfully had the Japanese used coconut logs, corrugated iron, steel beams, armor plate, concrete, coral rock, and sand in building their gun emplacements, dugouts, pillboxes, and blockhouses that they were almost immune to bombing and shelling. Little wonder that Betio's commander, Rear Admiral Keiji Shibasaki, boasted that the Americans could not conquer Tarawa "with a million men in a hundred years." Tides, coral reefs, and a picked garrison of more than 4000 Japanese Imperial Marines were thought to make Betio impregnable.

For three days Betio was blasted by naval shells and aerial bombs, but when the 2nd Marine Division hit the beaches on November 21, it met withering and accurate gunfire. Many landing craft were grounded on the fringing coral shoals and had to let Marines out to walk 700 yards through the water under murderous fire before they could get to the beaches. Carl Jonas, who fought there, describes the first-day landings on Tarawa:

The shore line curved like a longshoremen's hook,

A grim-faced Marine gunner tramps back after 19 days in the jungle.

Early landings led to jungles, but as the war moved north the Marines found

themselves on coral islands like Tarawa where there was little or no cover.

and the flat part to my right was the handle of it. From the other side, near the point of the hook, a Jap machine gun kept up a steady fire across our line of advance. Another machine gun was able to spit out almost directly at us, so that the two of them made a cross fire. Also, from some point I couldn't see, a mortar was dropping bursts ahead of us and slightly to our right. I saw no Marines on the beach, only blasted boats where they had stopped. Two of them were on fire. Beyond, a stout coconut-log barricade ran like a fence parallel to the whole shore. Then I got down as low as I could, with only my helmet showing, and began to crawl and duck-walk through the water, which was hardly three feet deep, even though we were almost a half mile out. I was heading for the right-hand flank, but just why, I couldn't say myself. . . .

I passed two or three dead Marines. My legs were very tired, and I couldn't keep my rifle out of the water. Finally, I used it to push myself along with, and forgot about keeping it dry. I saw a boat coming in toward me, and I worked away from it; for, although this brought me nearer the guns, I knew the boat would draw heavy fire, and wouldn't pick me up anyway. I kept down and pushed ahead, not very fast but steadily. Finally I came to what I though was the beach, but as I inched up onto it I saw it was a sand bar with another fifty yards of water on the other side. At the top were fifteen or twenty dead or wounded Marines. A man who had been in our boat crawled up beside me.

"Where are the other guys?" I asked him.

"I don't know," he said. "As soon as I find out, I'm going on in."

I didn't want to go over the sand bar very much, so I worked to the left, which again brought me closer to the fire, but gave me the cover provided by the water. I wondered if I was doing the right or the wrong thing. I decided it was more dangerous to stay still and think it out than to keep moving, so I just went on in. Then, just as I saw some Marines lying between the bar and the shore, a current caught me and carried me along with no bottom under my feet. I swam a few strokes and felt bottom again. My pack was heavy with water, so I slipped it off and, dragging it behind, scrambled up into the lee of the shore. It seemed like the sweetest earth this side of paradise, and I wanted to lie there forever without moving a muscle.

Of the 5000 men ashore by the end of D-Day, 1500 had been killed or wounded, and the rest were pinned down by Japanese gunfire on shallow beachheads. American shelling and bombing had not knocked out the Japanese defenses, but it had killed half the defenders and destroyed their communications so that no effective Japanese infiltration or counterattack could be mounted that first crucial night when the Marines on the beaches might have been pushed back into the lagoon.

The next day the Marines began the bloody job of taking each Japanese pillbox out, one by one, with grenades, demolition charges, and flame throwers. It took 76 hours of bitter, desperate fighting like that described by Robert Sherrod:

Not fifteen minutes later, in the same spot, I saw the most gruesome sight I had seen in this war. Another young Marine walked briskly along the beach. He grinned at a pal who was sitting next to me. Again there was a shot. The Marine spun all the way around and fell to the ground dead. From where he lay, a few feet away, he looked up at us. Because he had been shot squarely through the temple his eyes bulged out wide, as in horrific surprise at what had happened to

Seventh Division infantrymen use a flame thrower against a Japanese block-

him, though it was impossible that he could ever have known what hit him.

"Somebody go get that son-of-a-bitch," yelled Major Crowe. "He's right back of us here, just waiting for somebody to pass by." That Jap sniper, we knew from the crack of his rifle, was very close.

A Marine jumped over the seawall and began throwing blocks of fused TNT into a coconut-log pillbox about fifteen feet back of the seawall against which we sat. Two more Marines scaled the seawall, one of them carrying a twin-cylindered tank strapped to his shoul-

house on Kwajalein. Japanese troops fought to the end or committed suicide.

ders, the other holding the nozzle of a flame thrower. As another charge of TNT boomed inside the pillbox, causing smoke and dust to billow out, a khaki-clad figure ran out the side entrance. The flame thrower. waiting for him, caught him in its withering stream of intense fire. As soon as it touched him, the Jap flared up like a piece of celluloid. He was dead instantly but the bullets in his cartridge belt exploded for a full sixty seconds after he had been charred almost to nothingness. It was the first Jap I saw killed on Betio — the first of 4000.

By November 23, a thousand American Marines and sailors lay dead, 2100 were wounded, and the two-and-a-half miles length of Betio was secured. The Japanese fought almost to the last man; only 17 Japanese and 129 Koreans of the 4600-man garrison surrendered.

On Makin, 100 miles north of Betio, the Army's 27th Division had an easier time. Though outnumbering the Japanese 10–1, inexperience slowed the 27th up; but three days after landing, its commander declared: "Makin taken" with 200-odd casualties.

The Marshalls: Kwajalein and Eniwetok

With the experience of Tarawa under its belt, V 'Phib now prepared to invade the Marshall Islands, 500 miles northwest of the Gilberts, which the Japanese had held under League of Nations mandate since 1920. For two months before landing, carrier-based planes and land-based bombers from the Gilberts smashed shipping, defenses, planes, and airfields. The Japanese High Command, hard-pressed by Halsey and MacArthur's forces, could spare no help for the Marshalls. Bypassing the strongly fortified Japanese atolls with their smashed planes and neutralized airstrips, the Americans took the excellent harbor at Majuro Atoll unopposed, then hit strategic Kwajalein Atoll. The 4th Marine Division stormed ashore on the joined islands of Roi and Namur, the major Japanese base, in the northern part of Kwajalein Atoll, and in two days, by February 2, 1944, had secured them both. The Army's 7th Infantry Division had a harder time with Kwajalein Island, 44 miles south in the same atoll and the Marshalls' most important naval base, but after a week of ferocious Tarawa-like fighting, they had it mopped up by February 6.

Having bypassed Mille, Wotje, Maloelap, and Jaluit Atolls in the Marshalls, and left them to wither on the vine, the Americans a week later leapfrogged to Eniwetok Atoll, 326 miles northwest of Roi and only 669 miles from Truk. There, Marines and soldiers once again combined to take Engebi, Parry, and Eniwetok Islands in a savage contest from February 17 to 23.

The relatively light American casualties in the Marshalls resulted from applying the experiences bloodily learned at Tarawa. Preliminary naval shelling and aerial bombardment were increased; coordination of air support of troops and inshore naval gunfire were improved; amphibious assault craft were modified to meet the problems of coral reefs; rockets were added to the armament of ships and planes; and tactics and weapons for flushing die-hard Japanese out of their bunkers were perfected. The Marines at Tarawa had not died in vain.

Admiral Nimitz now concentrated on devastating Truk. With air fields in the Admiralties and the Marshalls, land-based bombers were within range of Truk and Admiral Mineichi Koga was forced to pull Japan's Combined Fleet out of its anchorage there and send it to the Palaus. A major air and sea strike by Admiral Spruance's fleet in mid-February pulverized Truk, sinking 2 light cruisers, 4 destroyers, 3 auxiliary cruisers, and many other warships in the harbor, and sending 24 merchant vessels to the bottom as well. From 250 to 275 Japanese planes were destroyed or damaged at a loss of only 17 planes. By spring 1944 Truk was almost neutralized and the outer ring of Japan's defenses had been pierced. The inner ring—the Marianas, Palaus, and Philippines—were still to come.

The bitter price of victory in the Pacific.

American infantrymen on Guam as the war moved toward Japan.

credits

THE PHOTOGRAPHS

THE WORDS

15-17
Fuchida, Mitsuo and Masatake Okumija (editors: Clarke Kawakami and Roger Pineau); from Midway: The Battle that Doomed Japan. © 1955 by U. S. Naval Institute, Annapolis, Md.

29-30
Haape, Heinrich and Dennis Henshaw; from Moscow Tram Stop. Collins Publishers, London; 4th November 1957; © 1962.

30-31
Werth, Alexander; from Leningrad. Hamish Hamilton Ltd., © 1944 by Alexander Werth. Reprinted by permission of the author.

33-37
Voyetkhov, Boris; from The Last Days of Sevastopol. © 1943 by Alfred A. Knopf, Inc. Reprinted by permission of the publisher.

40
Schroter, Heinz (translator: Constantine Fitzgibbon); from Stalingrad. © 1958

by E. P. Dutton & Co., Inc., translation © 1958 by Michael Joseph Ltd. Reprinted by permission of the publishers.
47-49
Zieser, Benno (translator: Alec Brown); from The Road to Stalingrad, Ballantine Books, Inc., published in England under the title In Their Shallow Graves. © 1956 by Benno Zieser, © Europa Verlag, Zurich. Reprinted by permission of the publisher and author.
56-60
Remy, Colonel; from Courage and Fear. Arthur Barker Ltd., London 1950. Reprinted by permission of the publisher and author.
65-67
Krabbe, Henning (editor); "Commando at St. Nazaire" from Voices from Britain. George Allen & Unwin, London, 1948. Reprinted by permission of the publisher.
67-69
Munro, Ross; from Gauntlet to Overlord. © 1945 by The Macmillan Co. of Canada Ltd. Reprinted by permission of the publisher.
76-79
Carse, Robert; from There Go the Ships. William Morrow & Co., © 1942 by Robert Carse. Reprinted by permission of Willis Kingsley Wing.
88-90
Johnston, George H.; from The Toughest Fighting in the World. Duell, Sloan & Pearce Inc., © 1943 by George H. Johnston. Reprinted by permission of the publisher, an affiliate of Meredith Press.
100-104
Leckie, Robert; from Helmet for My Pillow. Random House, Inc., © 1957 by Robert Hugh Leckie. Reprinted by permission of the publisher and the Sterling Lord Agency.
107-111
Samwell, H. P.; from An Infantry Officer with the Eighth Army. William Blackwood & Sons Ltd., 1945. Reprinted by permission of the publisher on behalf of the copyright holder.
132-133
Moorehead, Alan; from African Trilogy. Hamish Hamilton Ltd., 1945. Reprinted by permission of Laurence Pollinger Ltd.
141-145
von Mellenthin, F. W.; from Panzer Battles 1939-1945. © 1945 by the University of Oklahoma Press. Reprinted by permission of Cassell & Co. Ltd., London.
152-161
Belden, Jack; from Still Time to Die. Harper & Brothers, © 1944 by Jack Belden.
164
Wheeler, Sir Mortimer; from Still Digging. Michael Joseph Ltd., London; © 1955 by Sir Mortimer Wheeler. Reprinted by permission of the publisher and author.
170-176
Pyle, Ernie; from Brave Men. Holt, Rinehart & Winston, Inc., © 1943, 1944 by Scripps-Howard Newspaper Alliance, © 1944 by Holt, Rinehart & Winston, Inc. Reprinted by permission of the publisher.
190-193
White, Osmar; from Green Armour. W. W. Norton & Co., Inc., © 1945 by Osmar White. Reprinted by permission of the publisher.
200-205
Jonas, Carl; "The First Day of Tarawa" from The Saturday Evening Post, 1943. Curtis Publishing Co., © 1943 by Carl Jones. Reprinted by permission of the author and James Brown Associates, Inc.
205-207
Sherrod, Robert; from Tarawa. Duell, Sloan & Pearce, Inc., © 1944, 1945 by Robert Sherrod. Reprinted by permission of the publisher, an affiliate of Meredith Press.

"HITLER'S WAR"

From the German point of view and secret Nazi documents never before revealed to the public, here is the whole gigantic drama of the most crucial days of World War II. Bantam now presents the books that individually capture the major personalities and events of the war.

The world at your fingertips

Leading historians, sociologists, political scientists, economists, and anthropologists offer personal and political analyses of the world's developing lands.

☐ CHINA YESTERDAY AND TODAY
   Edited by Molly Joel Coye & Jon Livingston   2095 • $1.50

☐ THE ISRAEL-ARAB READER
   Edited by Walter Laqueur   2487 • $2.95

☐ JAPAN YESTERDAY AND TODAY
   Edited by Ray F. Downs   2884 • $1.50

☐ INDIA YESTERDAY AND TODAY
   Edited by Clark D. Moore & David Eldredge   7473 • $1.50

☐ LATIN AMERICA YESTERDAY AND TODAY
   Edited by John Rothchild   8348 • $1.25

Buy them at your local bookstore or use this handy coupon:

WE DELIVER!
And So Do These Bestsellers.

BOOKS BEHIND THE LINES:

The side of war you will never read about in the history books

☐	THE HOUSE ON GARIBALDI STREET Isser Harel	2501 •	$1.95
☐	THE WAR AGAINST THE JEWS Lucy S. Dawidowicz 1933-1945	2504 •	$2.50
☐	THE WALL John Hersey	2569 •	$2.25
☐	THE UPSTAIRS ROOM Johanna Reiss	2858 •	$1.25
☐	THE HIDING PLACE Corrie ten Boom	7903 •	$1.75
☐	THE PAINTED BIRD Jerzy Kosinski	8257 •	$1.75
☐	FAREWELL TO MANZANAR Jeanne Wakatsuki Houston and James D. Houston	8507 •	$1.25
☐	SUMMER OF MY GERMAN SOLDIER Bette Greene	10192 •	$1.50
☐	THE LAST OF THE JUST Andre Schwarz-Bart	10469 •	$1.95
☐	90 MINUTES AT ENTEBBE Dan Stevenson	10482 •	$1.95
☐	HIROSHIMA John Hersey	11077 •	$1.50

Buy them at your local bookstore or use this handy coupon for ordering:

Bantam Books, Inc., Dept. EDT, 414 East Golf Road, Des Plaines, Ill. 60016

Please send me the books I have checked above. I am enclosing $_____
(please add 50¢ to cover postage and handling). Send check or money order
—no cash or C.O.D.'s please.

Mr/Mrs/Miss_____

Address_____

City_____State/Zip_____

EDT-7/77

Please allow four weeks for delivery. This offer expires 7/78.

Bantam Book Catalog

Here's your up-to-the-minute listing of every book currently available from Bantam.

This easy-to-use catalog is divided into categories and contains over 1400 titles by your favorite authors.

So don't delay—take advantage of this special opportunity to increase your reading pleasure.

Just send us your name and address and 25¢ (to help defray postage and handling costs).

THE PHOTOGRAPHS: This volume includes such unforgettable photographs as: a lone German soldier desperately running for cover somewhere on the Russian front; an isolated American soldier guarding a howitzer position from his foxhole in Tunisia; a squad of American troops using a flamethrower in the action on Kwajalein; the touching portrait of a sobbing Italian girl and the thrilling scene of victorious Allied troops entering Palermo in Sicily.

THE WORDS: In this volume are Churchill's moving demand for unconditional surrender in June, 1943; the confident words of Montgomery and the arrogant taunts of Rommel. Here is Alan Moorehead's description of the 8th Army's joyous, flower-strewn march into Tunis, Ernie Pyle's brilliant report on the bitter Italian war and a Marine Sergeant's account of the bloody hand-to-hand fighting in Guadalcanal.

Eyewitness
History
Of
World
War II